Chinese Classics: Chinese-English Series

MENCIUS

Volume One

Chinese Classics : Chinese-English Series

MENCIUS
Volume One

Translated by
D.C. Lau

The Chinese University Press
Hong Kong

International Standard Book Number: 962-201-301-5

This book (without the accompanying Chinese text) was first published in 1979 by Penguin Books Ltd., Hamondsworth, Middlesex, England

The Chinese University Press
The Chinese University of Hong Kong
SHATIN, N. T., HONG KONG

Typesetting by
The Chinese University Press (English text)
Wonderful Typesetting Co. (Chinese text)
Printing by
Caritas Printing Training Centre

CONTENTS

NOTE ON BILINGUAL EDITION

In preparing the translation of the *Mencius* for this bilingual edition, I took the opportunity to give it a long overdue revision which, in the event, turned out to be more extensive than I had envisaged. Changes range from minor matters of wording to reinterpretation of the original text. In his article "On translating *Mencius*" (*Philosophy East and West*, Vol. XXX, 1, 1980, pp. 93-122), Professor David S. Nivison criticised certain passages in my translation. Where the criticisms are justified, in my revision I have taken account of them, but where there is room for a difference of opinion I have left the translation as it stood. In either case, I am grateful to Professor Nivison for having raised the points.

I have also taken this opportunity to reprint as a further appendix my article 'Some Notes on the *Mencius*' which first appeared in *Asia Major*, N. S. Vol. XV in 1969.

Hong Kong   D. C. L.
September, 1983

INTRODUCTION

Only two Chinese philosophers have the distinction of being known consistently to the West by a latinized name. The first is Confucius. The second is Mencius, whose name is Meng K'e. That Mencius should share the distinction is by no means an insignificant fact, for he is without doubt second only to Confucius in importance in the Confucian tradition, a fact officially recognized in China for over a thousand years. There are various reasons for this. First, the *Analects of Confucius* which forms almost the only reliable source of our knowledge of the thought of Confucius consists of a collection of sayings of the sage, mostly brief and often with little or no context. Hence many ideas are not elaborated upon, leaving a good deal of room for differences in interpretation. The *Mencius*, too, consists of sayings of Mencius and conversations he had with his contemporaries, but these tend to be of greater length and there is often some kind of a context. The ideas are, therefore, more articulate. Thus the *Mencius*, when read side by side with the *Analects of Confucius*, throws a great deal of light on the latter work. Second, Mencius developed some of the ideas of Confucius and at the same time discussed problems not touched on by Confucius. It is not an exaggeration to say that what is called Confucianism in subsequent times contains as much of the thought of Mencius as of Confucius.

The only other great name in early Confucianism is that of Hsün Tzu who was half a century or so later than Mencius. He developed Confucianism in a way radically different from that of Mencius, and we shall have occasion to mention him when we come to discuss the philosophical thought of Mencius. It is perhaps futile to try to decide which of the two was the greater thinker, as the difference between them is due mainly to a difference in philosophical temperament. In William James' famous distinction, Mencius is a 'tender-minded', and Hsün Tzu a 'tough-minded', philosopher. But Hsün Tzu had considerably less influence on subsequent thought than Mencius, and this for two reasons. First, Mencius was probably the greatest writer amongst ancient philosophers, while Hsün Tzu was, at best, the possessor of an indifferent literary style. When in T'ang times Han Yü raised the banner of the *ku wen* movement,[1] he looked to Mencius as much for his superb style as for his sound philosophy. Second, from the Sung onwards, the philosophy of Mencius

---

[1] The movement was so called because it advocated a return to *ku wen*, i.e., the prose style of the ancient period. This came about through a growing dissatisfaction with the parallel prose that had been prevalent since the Six Dynasties.

became the orthodoxy while Hsün Tzu was almost totally eclipsed. The *Great Learning*, the *Doctrine of the Mean*, the *Analects of Confucius*, together with the *Mencius*, became known as the *Four Books* which, until the present century, were read and memorized by every schoolboy in his first years at school. Thus the position and influence of Mencius were assured.

As with most ancient Chinese thinkers, little is known of the life of Mencius other than what we can glean from the work bearing his name. True, there is a biography[2] in the *Shih chi* (*Records of the Historian*), the first comprehensive history written at the beginning of the first century B.C., but this contains hardly any facts not to be found in the *Mencius* and when Ssu-ma Ch'ien departs from the *Mencius*, as in the case of dates, he goes wrong. There are also some early traditions concerning Mencius and his mother to be found in the *Han shih wai chuan* of the second century B.C. and the *Lieh nü chuan* just over a century later.[3] It is difficult to say how much credence can be given to these traditions, but they attained wide currency and great popularity as cautionary tales.

It is to the *Mencius*, therefore, that we must look if we wish to find out something about Mencius' life. The *Mencius* is divided into seven books, the titles of which are of no significance as they are all simply taken from the opening sentence of the books and, with the exception of the last book, are all names of persons with whom Mencius had conversations. There is no indication that any method for the grouping of the sections was followed by the editor, though Book V Part A, for instance, consists solely of questions and answers concerning history. There is, however, one exception, and that is Book I. There the sections are arranged chronologically, and it is this book that furnishes us with some precise dates. In I. A. 5, King Hui of Liang mentions his defeats by Ch'i to the east, by Ch'in to the west, and by Ch'u to the south. The defeat by Ch'i was at Ma Ling in 341 B.C. From that year onwards, for the next twenty years, Liang suffered a series of defeats at the hands of Ch'in. The humiliation inflicted by Ch'u was in 323 B.C. As King Hui died in 319 B.C., the meeting with Mencius must have fallen within the period, 323 to 319 B.C. With the death of King Hui, King Hsiang succeeded him and I. A. 6 records an interview with the new king. Mencius must have left Liang for Ch'i soon afterwards, finding King Hsiang lacking in the dignity befitting a king. In the next section we find a conversation with King Hsüan of Ch'i who had just succeeded his father, King Wei, in 320. The sections, from I. A. 7 to I. B. 11, are concerned with King Hsüan, and I. B. 10 and I. B. 11

---

[2] For a translation and a discussion of this biography see Appendix I.
[3] See Appendix 2.

both deal with the invasion of Yen by Ch'i in 314 B.C. This same event is also dealt with in II. B. 8 and II. B. 9, and this part of Book II seems also to be in chronological order. In II. B 14 we find Mencius explaining to a questioner that after his first meeting with the king he had no intention of staying in Ch'i, but 'it so happened that war broke out and I had no opportunity of requesting permission to leave'. This almost certainly refers to the war with Yen, and Mencius must have left shortly after hostilities came to an end. To return to Book I, the remaining chapters of the book record conversations with Duke Mu of Tsou, Duke Wen of T'eng and finally with Duke P'ing of Lu. It seems likely that after he left Ch'i Mencius stopped in Tsou and T'eng on his way to Lu. We know nothing of Mencius after this. He probably lived out his last years in retirement in Lu.

There are various events in the *Mencius* with no clear indication of date: for instance, Mencius' return to Lu to bury his mother (II. B. 7), and conversations he had with Duke Wen of T'eng and with his envoys (III. A. 1 to III. A. 3). These, it seems to me, can be fitted into the period 319-314 B.C., for during this period, although Mencius was staying in Ch'i, he made trips abroad from time to time. We know, at least, of one occasion when he was sent as official envoy to the funeral of Duke Ting of T'eng, the father of Duke Wen (II. B. 6). There is no convincing evidence,[4] as far as one can see, for any events recorded in the *Mencius* happening before 319 B.C.

Although we know the dates of the visit to Liang and Ch'i, there is still the question of Mencius' age at that time. There is no direct evidence for a clear answer to this question, but there is some indication that Mencius was an old man. Twice King Hui used the word *sou* (old man) in talking to Mencius. If we bear in mind the fact that the king himself was a man of about seventy, it is unlikely that Mencius was very much younger.

If what we have said so far is accepted, then the *Mencius* covers the last years of Mencius' life. This would mean that the views expressed in the work are his mature views and represent the fruits of a lifetime spent in reflection and teaching. It would also account for the consistency of the work and the authority with which Mencius speaks and, perhaps, for the superb literary skill with which he expresses his ideas.

It is within the fourth century B.C. that the whole of Mencius' life falls, and the fourth century B.C. saw some radical and far-reaching changes in China. The feudal system was gradually replaced by a system of centralized government under which the state was divided into administrative districts. The sale and purchase of land came to be permitted and tax on land was levied in kind. A number of states began to put into practice ideas of Legalist

---

[4] For a discussion of the evidence see Appendix I.

philosophers aimed at strengthening the state. The goal was a highly centralized government with laws applied equally stringently to everyone in the state, and ultimately at a healthy agrarian economy with every peasant able to take up arms in time of war. There is no doubt that the application of these policies brought short-term success, as these states were able, because of their increased military strength, to expand at the expense of their more conservative neighbours. This process culminated in the unification of China in 221 B.C. by the state of Ch'in which was most thoroughgoing in its adoption of Legalist ideas. But this was to come. In Mencius' time it meant more frequent wars on an ever-increasing scale. It also meant a growing cynicism towards morality which is implicit in Legalist doctrines based on a view of man as purely egoistic and motivated solely by the thought of reward and punishment. With the prevalent trends Mencius was totally out of sympathy. In his view man is basically a moral creature. To understand this we must take a brief look at the roots of his thought.

In reading the Mencius one cannot but be struck by the admiration shown by Mencius for Confucius, and there is no doubt that Mencius' philosophy is essentially based on the teachings of Confucius, though in some respects it developed beyond their limits, mainly because philosophical problems had arisen since Confucius of which any serious thinker had to take cognizance.

As Mencius admired Confucius, so did Confucius admire the Duke of Chou. Now when the Chou replaced the Yin as the ruling house of the Empire, they expounded a philosophy as much to instil resignation in the conquered as to inculcate a self-searching vigilance in themselves. To the conquered they had to explain the reason for their loss of the Empire. The Yin believed that they ruled by virtue of the Mandate of Heaven, and because they had held it for so long they had forgotten that this Mandate could be withdrawn. The Chou, by wresting the Empire from the Yin, had shown this to be the case, and they reiterated this truth; this is summed up in a line in the *Odes*.

The Mandate of Heaven is not immutable.[5]

A ruling house could retain the Mandate only so long as it acted morally, that is, acted solely with the good of the people at heart. It would lose it, as indeed the Yin lost it, if the Emperor strayed from the path of virtue. Now this doctrine was double-edged. If it explained the fall of the Yin, it also laid down the conditions which must constantly be fulfilled if the Chou were to retain the Mandate. Hence the Chou Emperors were warned that they had to be constantly vigilant over their own conduct. There is no doubt that the Duke of Chou was the architect of this philosophy and it is easy to understand the

[5] Ode 235. Mencius quotes this ode in IV. A. 7.

admiration shown by Confucius.

Confucius' most distinctive contribution to Chinese thought is his exposition of the concepts of *jen* and *yi*. *Jen* has been variously rendered in English as benevolence, human-heartedness, goodness, love, altruism and humanity. Of these I think benevolence is the least objectionable, and as far as Mencius is concerned, has the advantage of echoes of Bishop Butler. For Butler, both benevolence and self-interest are principles as distinct from particular passions, and there is something of this distinction in the thought of Mencius. *Yi* is often rendered as righteousness, but this, though close enough as an equivalent, lacks the versatility of the Chinese word. *Yi* can be applied to an act which is right, to the agent who does what is right and to a duty which an agent ought to do. Although both *jen* and *yi* are of the first importance to Confucius' teaching, *jen* is more basic. It is the totality of moral virtues and, looked at from this point of view, we can say that *yi* is rooted in *jen*. As we shall see, both *jen* and *yi* figure prominently in Mencius' teaching and he gave *jen* an important place in his political philosophy.

We have already remarked on the fact that although Mencius thought of himself as a successor to Confucius, nevertheless, because of the changes in the philosophical scene, he had to deal with problems which were either unknown or unimportant in Confucius' day. Mencius' name is, above all, associated with his theory of the goodness of human nature. Now the only remark made by Confucius on the subject is that 'men are close to one another by nature and they diverge as a result of practice' (the *Analects of Confucius*, XVII. 2). That there is only one somewhat non-committal remark in the whole of the *Analects of Confucius* on human nature shows at least that human nature was not a prominent issue in the day of Confucius. By contrast, it must have been a hotly debated topic in Mencius' day. Let us look at the factors contributing to the complexity of the problem.

The concept of *ming*, which in the early Chou was essentially the *mandate* given by Heaven to the ruling house, has meantime undergone development in two ways. Although *ming* had always meant the moral commands of Heaven, so long as it was conceived of as affecting only the fortunes of Empires, there was no need to deal with the relationship between human nature and the mandate of Heaven. But in the course of time the concept of *ming* was extended. The individual, too, has his *ming*. He, too, is enjoined by Heaven to be moral. The question then arises, given his nature, can he obey the commands of Heaven? The answer to this question depends, of course, on the view of human nature one holds. The second development is that *ming* gradually took on the meaning of destiny. Already in the *Analects of Confucius* we find examples of this use of the word (e.g. XII. 5). This is even more inimical to moral teachings. If what will be will be, there is hardly room left for human effort, let alone morality. Now by Mencius' time, there was a theory of human nature which must have been widely accepted. According to this theory, the nature of a man consists of his desires and appetites, a view summed up in Kao Tzu's remark, 'Appetite for food and sex is nature' (VI. A. 4). If this were true, man has no other motive to action than the urge to find gratification for his desires, and no matter how much he may wish to comply with the commands of Heaven, it is impossible for him to do so.

It is against this background that we must approach Mencius' theory of human nature. First of all, let us dispose of certain misunderstandings. It has been said by interpreters that Mencius put forth his theory solely with sages in mind, as the sage is the only type of man who possesses unadulterated goodness. This is to restrict the application of Mencius' theory to a small section of humanity, but as Mencius makes it quite clear that his theory is meant to apply universally to all men, there must be something wrong with the interpretation.

Mencius nowhere contradicted Kao Tzu's statement that 'appetite for food and sex is nature'. He would proabbly admit that desires and appetites form the greater part of human nature. What he emphatically denied was that human nature consisted *solely* of desires and appetites. According to him, 'Slight is the difference between man and the brutes. The common man loses this distinguishing feature, while the gentleman retains it' (IV. B. 19). To say that the difference between man and the brutes is slight is to imply that they are, for the most part, the same, and if the nature of animals consists solely of desires and appetites, then these must also make up the greater part of human nature. There is, however, a difference, and this, though slight, sets man apart from the animals. Whether a man is a gentleman or not depends on whether he succeeds in retaining and, we may say, developing this difference. But what is this distinguishing feature that the gentleman retains? The answer is, it is his heart (*hsin*). In IV. B. 28, Mencius says, 'A gentleman differs from other men in that he retains his heart.' This 'retaining of the heart' is again mentioned in VII. A. 1. It is necessary to emphasize the retention of the heart because it is something very easy to lose. Since the heart is something we possess originally, it is also referred to as the 'original heart'. Mencius describes a man who loses his sense of shame and comes to do things for unworthy motives which he would not, in the first instance, have done even to escape death as a man who has lost his 'original heart' (VI. A. 10). Mencius also calls it the 'true heart'. It is not the case that a man never possessed the benevolent and righteous heart, but that he has 'let go of his true heart' (VI. A. 8). We are said to 'let go' of the heart because we possessed it in the first place. The purpose of learning is 'to go after this strayed heart' (VI. A. 11).

What, we may ask, is the special function of the heart? The answer, according to Mencius, is that it is the function of the heart to think. This marks it off from the other parts of the person, particularly the senses. These, being unable to think, are drawn blindly to the objects of their desires. The eyes are attracted by beautiful sights and the ear to beautiful sounds. This is, in principle, no different from one inanimate object being attracted by another, for instance, iron being attracted by a loadstone. Hence man, if he puts aside his heart, is attracted by outside things as one thing by another. 'The organs of hearing and sight are unable to think and can be misled by external things,' says Mencius. 'When one thing acts on another, all it does is to attract it. The organ of the heart can think. But it will find the answer only if it does think; otherwise, it will not find the answer. This is what Heaven has given me' (VI. A. 15). We can see from this passage why Mencius attaches the greatest importance to the heart. Without the ability to think, a living creature is completely determined by its desires and the desires are totally at the mercy of their respective objects. It is the gift from Heaven of a thinking heart that marks human beings off from animals, but, Mencius warns, the mere possession of the heart is not enough, we must in fact think with it. If we fail to make use of the heart, we are still no different from animals.

What was it Mencius had in mind when he talked about thinking? He had in mind moral thinking — thinking about moral duties, about priorities, about the purpose and destiny of man and his position in the universe. For Mencius, intellectual thinking forms an insignificant part of thinking. This was a feature common to all ancient Chinese thought. Let us look a little more closely at the objects of thought.

In a group of sections in Book VI Part A, Mencius deals with the problem of relative value. According to this, the various members of the human person are not of equal value. The heart is a greater member while the sense organs are lesser members. A greater member is higher than a lesser member. The difference between a great man and a small man lies in the priorities they give to these members. The great man gets his priorities right, while the small man gets them wrong. The latter is described as 'unthinking to the highest degree' (VI. A. 13).

We can see that the function of the heart being to think, it can make judgements on the relative value of the different members of the human person including itself, and further that it is in fact the heart itself that is of the highest value. This ties up with what Mencius says elsewhere. 'Reason and rightness please my heart in the same way as meat pleases my palate' (VI. A. 7). What pleases the heart is of higher value than what pleases the senses.

Now we are in a better position to appreciate Mencius' objections to the views of human nature current in his day, and also the distinctive feature of his own theory. Though one may admit that man shares with animals the possession of appetites and desires and though one may further admit that these form the greater part of his make-up, nevertheless, one is justified in saying that the desireful nature of man cannot be called human nature, because this fails to distinguish him from animals. What distinguishes him from animals is his heart, for though this forms but a small part of his nature it is both unique to man and the highest amongst his bodily organs.

It is worthwhile at this point to mention one feature of the view of man held by Mencius and, indeed, by Chinese thinkers in general. There is no bifurcation of man into soul and body as in the Western tradition, and so the problem of how the two can interact does not arise. Man, for Mencius, is an organic whole, though in the complex structure which is his person we can distinguish the higher constituents from the lower. It is for this reason that in Mencius' view what is wrong with a man who cares only for his belly is merely that he has got his priorities wrong. If he gets these right, then there is nothing wrong with caring for the belly. He says, 'If a man who cares about food and drink can do so without neglecting any other part of his person, then his mouth and belly are much more than just a foot or an inch of his skin' (VI. A. 14). Again, according to him, a healthy heart in a man 'manifests itself in his face, giving it a sleek appearance. It also shows in his back and extends to his limbs, rendering their message intelligible without words' (VII. A. 21). Finally, he says, 'Our body and complexion are given to us by Heaven. Only a sage can give his body complete fulfilment' (VII. A. 38).

So far we have only seen that the heart is pleased by what is right and reasonable, but the essentially moral nature of the heart is much more deep-seated than that. According to Mencius, there are four incipient tendencies in the heart. These he calls 'the heart of compassion', 'the heart of shame', 'the heart of courtesy and modesty', and 'the heart of right and wrong' (II. A. 6 and VI. A. 6). Mencius further points out that 'the heart of compassion' is the germ of benevolence; 'the heart of shame', the germ of dutifulness; 'the heart of courtesy and modesty', the germ of the observance of the rites; and, 'the heart of right and wrong', the germ of wisdom (II. A. 6). Each of these four tendencies has its own significance. The heart of compassion, the finding of suffering in others unbearable, if naturally found in all human beings, will show, according to Mencius, that benevolence has a basis in human nature, and benevolence is the strongest motive to moral action. On the heart of shame Mencius places the greatest emphasis. 'A man,' says Mencius, 'must not be without shame, for the shame of being without shame is shamelessness indeed' (VII. A. 6). Again, he says, 'Great is the use of shame to man. He who indulges in craftiness has no use for shame. If a man is not ashamed of being inferior to other men, how will he ever become their equal?' (VII. A. 7). A man's aspirations to become a morally better man are founded on his feeling of shame. Unless a man realizes his own inferiority, he cannot be expected to make any effort, and not to realize one's own moral inferiority is the greatest obstacle to moral progress. 'When one's finger is inferior to other people's, one has sense enough to resent it, but not when one's heart is inferior. This is what is called a lack of knowledge of priorities. (VI. A. 12). The importance of shame is summed up in the following words 'Only when a man will not do some things is he capable of doing great things' (IV. B. 8).

'The heart of courtesy and modesty' describes both a man's modesty which does not allow him to claim credit and the courtesy that prompts him to yield precedence to others. This is the basis of rules of conduct in polite society. In a sense, this is a curb on one's natural self-seeking tendencies, and, as we shall see, the clear distinction between morality and self-interest is the corner-stone of Confucian moral theory.

Finally, 'the heart of right and wrong' has a twofold significance. First, it refers to the ability of the heart to distinguish between right and wrong. Second, it can also refer to the approval of the right and the disapproval of the wrong by the heart. Now this ability of the heart is relevant to the under-standing of the reasons for Mencius' holding the view that human nature is good. For even when we fail to do what is right we cannot help seeing that what we have failed to do is right and feeling disapproval towards the course of action we have chosen, with its accompanying sense of shame. In this way the statement that human nature is good is given a sense which is completely independent of the way in which human beings in fact behave. Those who think that Mencius, in formulating his theory, had only sages in mind have failed utterly to understand him.

Mencius simply states that there are these four tendencies in man. He does not go on to make any attempt to show that this is so, except in the case of 'the heart of compassion'. In a justly famous passage, he says:

> Suppose a man were, all of a sudden, to see a young child on the verge of falling into a well. He would certainly be moved to compassion, not because he wanted to get in the good graces of the parents, nor because he wished to win the praise of his fellow villagers or friends, nor yet because he disliked the cry of the child. (II. A. 6).

This passage contains a number of points crucial to Mencius' theory, and it is worth looking at it in some detail.

The first point is that the feeling of compassion experienced by the man who saw the child creeping towards the well is completely disinterested. For if his feeling had been motivated by self-interest, he would most likely have acted from one of the motives which Mencius expressly excluded, viz. the hope of getting in the good graces of the child's parents or of winning the praise of his fellow villagers or friends, or even the desire to stop the cry of the child which he found unpleasant. As he had none of these things in mind, he was unlikely to have acted from any other selfish motive. Mencius clinches the argument by deliberately putting in the qualification 'all of a sudden'. The reaction was instantaneous, and therefore spontaneous, as there was no time to reflect, and a reaction which is spontaneous is a true manifestation of a man's nature, because he is caught off his guard.

The second point is that Mencius has taken care not to overstate his case. All men have such a tendency to compassion, but this is literally the germ of benevolence and no more. In order to develop this into full-fledged benevolence, a great deal of nurturing is required. We may notice that the man is only said to experience a feeling of pity. Nothing is said about his taking any action. We are not even told how long the feeling lasted. It may be just a momentary twinge. For as soon as the man gets over the 'suddenness' of the situation his usual habits of thought are liable to reassert themselves. Indeed, calculating thoughts of self-interest probably arise in his mind and he may raise the question of whether it is worth his while to do anything about the child at all. But whatever happens afterwards, the fact remains that he had no control over the momentary twinge he felt in the first instance and that is all Mencius needs to show that the man has the germ of morality in him. It is for this reason that Mencius says that human nature is good, for no one is completely devoid of such feeling no matter how faint and momentary the experience proves to be. It is also for this reason that Mencius says that the difference between man and animals is slight. It lies in these incipient moral tendencies which are easily lost and such a loss is tantamount to the loss of one's 'original heart'.

At this point it is convenient to compare Mencius' theory of the goodness of human nature with the theory of Hsün Tzu that human nature is bad; for the precise way in which the two philosophers differ has often been misunderstood. It is often assumed that the two theories are contradictory in the same way as, for instance, to say of one and the same thing that it is both white and black. This can be seen from the fact that it is often said that whereas Mencius, in putting forth his theory, had only sages in mind, Hsün Tzu, on the other hand, had in mind only totally wicked men. But to do so is to forget that Mencius and Hsün Tzu shared one common belief, and that is that all men are capable of becoming sages. In other words, Mencius did not think that the failure of men to act morally, at least at times, invalidated his theory, while Hsün Tzu equally did not see any contradiction between his theory together with the fact that few men succeed in becoming sages and his belief that all men are capable of doing so.

What then is Hsün Tzu's theory that human nature is bad? And on what grounds is it based? Hsün Tzu believed that human nature, in concrete terms, consists of certain factors which, in response to outside things, manifest themselves as desires. If every man gives full rein to his desires, the result is certain to be conflict. There are two reasons for this. There are some things which are scarce and will fall short of the quantity necessary to satisfy the desire of all men for them. Even where there is no scarcity, there may still be conflict if more than one man desire one and the same object. Given Hsün Tzu's characterization of human nature, conflict is inevitable, and as conflict is the one thing which, in Hsün Tzu's view, is unquestionably bad, it follows that human nature inevitably leads to a state of affairs which is bad. Whatever necessarily leads to consequences that are bad is itself bad. Hence, concludes Hsün Tzu, human nature is bad.

Hsün Tzu's problem is, then, how to find a way out of this human predicament. His solution is morality, which he conceives of as a system of rules according to which what every man is entitled to is clearly laid down. If one's status does not entitle one to the possession of a thing, even if the thing is in plentiful supply and one has the money, one is still not permitted to possess it.

The solution is purely a theoretical one, and Hsün Tzu has still to show its practicability. First, in Hsün Tzu's view, the solution was arrived at by the ancient sages, but once invented it was obvious to anyone with average intelligence. In this respect it is somewhat like the way Columbus stood an egg on its end. Second, the ancient sages also saw the feasibility of the solution. The basis of the feasibility of the solution lies in habituation. A man can be trained to behave invariably in a way which is contrary to his nature: habit can become second nature. But how can a man make a beginning? This is possible, according to Hsün Tzu, because of the function of the heart. He draws a distinction between the desire for a thing and positive action to go after it. Although Hsün Tzu admits that the heart can never stop a man from desiring a thing, it can, however, make him desist from going after it. One does not go after an object once it is shown to be impossible to secure, a judgement only the heart can make. Similarly, a man can be made by his heart to make an effort to go after a thing when he has no desire for it, or to make a greater effort than is warranted by the strength of his desire.

Now the ancient sages, in inventing morality, saw not only that their solution, once pointed out would appear to be obviously reasonable to the hearts of all men, but also that all men could be conditioned to become moral against their nature, because the heart has, as we have seen, certain control over action, though not over desires.

An obvious question arises: why does Hsün Tzu exclude the heart from

human nature and so look upon morality as contrary to what is natural? This
is due to his definition of 'nature'. In order for a characteristic to count as
part of the nature of a thing, it must be inseparable from that thing, impossible
to learn to do or to get to do better through application. An example would
be the ability of the eye to see. This can be considered part of the nature of
the eye, because it cannot be separated from the eye. An eye that cannot see
is not, properly speaking, an eye at all. Further, seeing is not something we
can learn and we do not improve our ability to see through application.

This is not true of the heart, nor of morality which is the invention of the
heart. Not every man but only the ancient sages had the capacity to invent
morality, and moral behaviour has to be inculcated into a man. Even then
success is by no means assured.

We can see now that Mencius and Hsün Tzu took a very different line in
the matter of the definition of the nature of a thing. Mencius was looking for
what is distinctive while Hsün Tzu was looking for what forms an inseparable
part of it. For this reason, desires do not qualify, for Mencius, as a defining
characteristic of the nature of man because they are shared with animals. The
heart, and in particular the incipient moral tendencies in the human heart, is
what distinguishes a man from animals, and as such is a higher organ than his
senses. For Hsün Tzu, on the other hand, only what is instinctive can be
counted as nature, and the heart with its varying possibilities disqualifies
itself.

So far, we have only given an account of the difference between Mencius
and Hsün Tzu in terms of the difference in their attitude towards the matter
of definition. There are, of course, real differences as well. For Hsün Tzu
morality is purely an artificial way of behaviour. True, there must always have
existed a possibility, and it is this possibility that prompted the sages to invent
morality as a way out of the human predicament. But there is a wide gulf
between the possible and the natural. To borrow an illustration from an
argument between Mencius and Kao Tzu, it is possible to bend a willow into a
cup in the sense that it is impossible to bend a stone. Nevertheless, from
Mencius' standpoint, it is not natural for a willow to be bent into a cup in the
sense that it is natural for trees to grow on a mountain. Morality is natural in
this sense. The incipient moral tendencies are there in human nature originally.
They may be weak and easily destroyed, but this does not make them any
less natural. According to Hsün Tzu this is not so. Morality is a possible
solution to the problem of human conflict but it forms no part of original
human nature. This can be shown by the fact that it is separable from man. If
we bear in mind that Confucian morality demands of a man his willingness to
lay down his life for the sake of morality, we are likely to feel that in the
final test the gentleman as conceived by Hsün Tzu may be found wanting. It

is doubtful if habit, no matter how strong, will enable a man to walk to the scaffold for the sake of his duty.

To go back to Mencius: the emphasis on a natural moral motive, as distinct from one based on self-interest in the case of the man who sees a child creeping towards a well, touches on a basic tenet of Confucian thought—the distinction between morality and self-interest. The difference between a gentleman and a small man is that the former pursues morality with single-minded dedication while the latter pursues profit with equally single-minded dedication. (VII. A. 25) There is never any doubt in Mencius' mind that when self-interest comes into conflict with morality, it is self-interest that should give way. 'Life is what I want; dutifulness is also what I want. If I cannot have both, I would rather take dutifulness than life' (VI. A. 10). Confucius is also quoted as saying, 'A man whose mind is set on high ideals never forgets that he may end in a ditch; a man of valour never forgets that he may forfeit his head' (II. B. 1 and V. B. 7). This may give the wrong impression that self-interest and morality are necessarily opposed. This is certainly not the Confucian position, which is rather that the two are totally unconnected. It is only when self-interest becomes an obstacle to morality that the former has to be sacrificed, and it is perhaps true that self-interest is the most likely culprit against morality. But nevertheless when self-interest is not in conflict with morality a man has a duty to be prudent. He should not, for instance, stand under a wall on the verge of collapse (VII. A. 2).

There is a difference between self-interest and morality which is relevant to a problem that we touched upon earlier. We pointed out that *ming* gradually took on the meaning of 'Destiny'. There are examples of the word used in this sense even in the *Analects of Confucius* (see, for example, XII. 5). It should, however, be pointed out that the fatalism that was accepted by the Confucianist was of a limited kind. Only life and death, wealth and position are said to depend on Destiny. This is to get men to see that it is futile to pursue such ends, ends that most people devote most of their time and energy to. If these things depend on Destiny, then there is no point in pursuing them. What we ought to pursue is morality which is our proper end. On this matter Mencius has this to say:

Seek and you will get it; let go and you will lose it. If this is the case, then seeking is of use for getting and what is sought is within yourself. But if there is a proper way to seek it and whether you get it or not depends on Destiny, then seeking is of no use to getting and what is sought lies outside yourself. (VII. A. 3)

When whether we are going to get a thing or not depends on Destiny and our seeking makes no difference to our success or otherwise, then obviously there is no point in seeking it and if we seek it at all, we must do so in accordance with what is right. Mencius seems to intend that all external possessions should come under this head. The only things that are left which we have a duty to seek because seeking makes a difference to our success are internal things. These are our original heart and, more generally, moral ends. In these cases seeking helps because, in a sense, the seeking *is* the getting. Being moral does not depend on successful results but simply on our making the effort. As Confucius put it, 'Is benevolence really far away? No sooner do I desire benevolence than it is here' (*Analects of Confucius*, VII. 30). Thus we can see that fatalism of the kind advocated by Confucianists does not constitute an obstacle to obeying Heaven's decree that man should be moral.

Let us return to the subject of incipient moral tendencies. We have seen that, according to Mencius, a man naturally has these tendencies but they are easily smothered and need a great deal of care and cultivation. But how is this done? On this question Mencius has a great deal to say. One great difference between moral philosophers in the Chinese tradition and those in the Western tradition is that the latter do not look upon it as their concern to help people to become sages while the former assume that that is their main concern. Western philosophers deal only with the problem of what morality is. They leave the problem of how to make people better to religious teachers. In China, however, there has never been a strong tradition of religious teaching, and the problem has always fallen within the province of the philosopher.

To understand Mencius' teaching on the matter, it is necessary first to say something about the cosmology prevalent in the fourth century B.C. It was believed that the universe was made up of *ch'i* but this *ch'i* varied in consistency. The grosser *ch'i*, being heavy, settled to become the earth, while the refined *ch'i*, being light, rose to become the sky. Man, being half-way between the two, is a harmonious mixture of the two kinds of *ch'i*. His body consists of grosser *ch'i* while his heart is the seat of the refined *ch'i*. The blood, being neither as solid as the body nor as refined as the breath, lies somewhere in between, but as it is not static and circulates in the body it is more akin to the refined *ch'i*. Hence the term *hsüeh ch'i* (blood and *ch'i*). It is in virtue of the refined *ch'i* that a man is alive and his faculties can function properly. As the heart is the seat of this refined *ch'i*, it is necessary to have a regimen for the heart in order to be healthy and to live to a ripe old age.

Now there seemed to be two schools of thought on this matter. According to one school, though one is born with a fixed fund of *ch'i*, it is possible to acquire further supplies of it, and it is through the apertures that the *ch'i* enters the body. But whether the *ch'i* will stay once it has entered depends on whether the heart is in a fit state for it to take up abode. In order to be a fit abode the heart must be clean, that is, unclouded by desires. The other school believed that the original fund of *ch'i* cannot be replenished, and one dies when it is used up. The possibility of prolonging life lies in good husbandry of what one is endowed with. Every mental activity uses up a certain amount of *ch'i*. Excessive concentration of the heart in thought or the senses on external objects will unnecessarily speed up this expenditure. Hence the slogan of this school is: keep your apertures shut. This is directly opposite to the other school whose object is to let more *ch'i* in and whose slogan is: keep your apertures open.

In a well-known passage in II. A. 2, Mencius describes what he calls the *hao jan chih ch'i* (the flood-like *ch'i*), and it is obvious that this presupposes the prevalent theory we have outlined. For instance, not only does Mencius say of the *ch'i* that it 'fills the body',[6] but it is also impossible to understand his illustration of how the heart is moved by the *ch'i*, that is, how 'stumbling and hurrying affect the *ch'i*, yet in fact palpitations of the heart are produced', unless we understand the '*ch'i*' here as the breath which is supposed to fill the body.

But Mencius did not simply take over the current theory of *ch'i*, he gave it a twist. In place of the physical *ch'i* he puts his own *hao jan chih ch'i* 'which is, in the highest degree, vast and unyielding'. The point of contact between the *hao jan chih ch'i* and physical *ch'i* is courage. Courage is believed to depend on *ch'i*.[7] This no doubt has something to do with the fact that courage is accompanied by a state of heightened tension in the body in which breathing is quickened and the activity of the heart stimulated. But for Mencius genuine courage, instead of being sustained by a state of heightened tension in the body, can only be sustained by the sense of being morally in the right. The *hao jan chih ch'i* 'is a *ch'i* which unites rightness and the Way. Deprive it of these and it will collapse.' As Tseng Tzu put it, 'If, on looking within, one finds oneself to be in the wrong, then even though one's adversary be only a common fellow coarsely clad one is bound to tremble with fear. But if one finds oneself in the right, one goes forward even against men in the thousands.'

In order to become a good man, it is this *hao jan chih ch'i* that one must cultivate. 'Nourish it with integrity and place no obstacle in its path and it will fill the space between Heaven and Earth.' Elsewhere, Mencius describes the gentleman as being 'in the same stream as Heaven above and Earth below' (VII. A. 13). If we remember that it is Heaven which planted the moral heart

---

[6] This is almost identical with a similar statement in chapter 37 (13. 4b) of the *Kuan tzu*, the only difference being that in the *Kuan tzu*, the word used for 'body' is *shen* instead of *t'i*.

[7] The morale of an army is, for instance, called *shih ch'i*, that is, the *ch'i* of the soldiers.

in man, it is hardly surprising that man is in the same stream as Heaven when his heart is cultivated to its utmost possibility.

On the cultivation of one's moral character, there is one important and eloquent passage in which Mencius compares the heart to a mountain:

> There was a time when the trees were luxuriant on the Ox Mountain. As it is on the outskirts of a great metropolis, the trees are constantly lopped by axes. Is it any wonder that they are no longer fine? With the respite they get in the day and in the night, and the moistening by the rain and dew, there is certainly no lack of new shoots coming out, but then the cattle and sheep come to graze upon the mountain. That is why it is as bald as it is. People, seeing only its baldness, tend to think that it never had any trees. But can this possibly be the nature of a mountain? Can what is in man be completely lacking in moral inclinations? A man's letting go of his true heart is like the case of the trees and the axes. When the trees are lopped day after day, is it any wonder that they are no longer fine? If, in spite of the respite a man gets in the day and in the night and of the effect of the morning air on him, scarcely any of his likes and dislikes resembles those of other men, it is because what he does in the course of the day once again dissipates what he has gained. If this dissipation happens repeatedly, then the influence of the air in the night will no longer be able to preserve what was originally in him, and when that happens, the man is not far removed from an animal. Others, seeing his resemblance to an animal, will be led to think that he never had any native endowment. But can that be what a man is genuinely like? Hence, given the right nourishment there is nothing that will not grow, while deprived of it there is nothing that will not wither away. Confucius said, 'Hold on to it and it will remain; let go of it and it will disappear. One never knows the time it comes or goes, neither does one know the direction'. It is perhaps to the heart this refers. (VI. A. 8)

The comparison of the heart to a mountain is more than just an analogy. There is something which the two share in common. Just as it is natural for trees to grow on a mountain, so it is natural for moral shoots in the heart to develop into full-fledged moral tendencies. In the case of the mountain, it is the constant lopping of the trees by axes and eating away of young shoots by sheep and cattle that reduce it to a hopeless barrenness. Similarly, it is through pre-occupation with selfish thought and deed that a man's natural tendencies are destroyed. Even then there are moral shoots that come up, just as there are new shoots coming up in the case of the mountain, and it is only when these are repeatedly destroyed that the man is reduced hopelessly to the level of animals. Thus it can be seen that morality is natural to man in the sense that moral shoots spring up naturally when a man is left alone, just as new shoots spring up on the soil when the mountain is left alone. The use of axes and the grazing by sheep and cattle are artificial and accidental to the mountain. Similarly, the selfish desires which destroy a man's moral tendencies do not constitute his essential nature. Furthermore, what gives nourishment to the soil on the mountain is the respite it gets in the night and the moistening by the rain and the dew. Similarly, it is the rest in the night and the reviving power of the air in the night and the early morning which give nourishment to the moral shoots that will spring up naturally if only given the chance. Here Mencius is doing more than giving us a metaphorical account of the moral tendencies in a man. He is in fact giving us a practical touchstone for gauging our own moral progress. The freshness and spontaneity a man feels in the morning after a good night's rest constitute the best conditions for preserving and developing his true heart. Perhaps Mencius implies that moral health is inseparable from mental health. Whether this is so or not, a man can see that he is making moral progress in so far as he is able to hold on to this state of mind further and further into the day without its being dissipated by the distraction of selfish thoughts and deeds. It is worth mentioning in this connexion that the Confucian tradition believes in the joy of being a good man. Both Confucius and Mencius repeatedly use the phrase 'delighting in the Way'. Once more this emphasizes the naturalness of morality. Delight and joy are usually experienced when a man pursues a natural activity unimpeded. On this point one can see that Hsün Tzu is not in the true tradition of Confucius, as he looks upon morality as artificial and therefore unnatural. A man, according to him, can only learn to behave morally through incessant habituation over a lengthy period of time. This may, indeed, change a man to a moral automaton, but one cannot see how he can feel joy in the pursuance of an automatic activity.

Now that we have completed the account of Mencius' theory that human nature is good, let us go back to the question which Mencius must have been faced with at the outset: if human nature is nothing but desires, how can man possibly obey the Decree of Heaven? The answer, as we have seen, is in two stages. First, human nature is defined in terms of what is unique to man, viz., his heart, rather than in terms of desires which he shares with animals. Second, the human heart has built-in moral tendencies which though incipient can be developed, and when fully developed will enable a man to become a sage. In this way acting morally is no longer an obedience to an external command, even though the command may issue from Heaven. Acting in accordance with Heaven's Decree is something one can do joyfully by looking inwards and finding the roots of morality within one's own spiritual make-up. In this way, Mencius broke down the barrier between Heaven and Man and between the Decree and human nature. There is a secret passage leading from the innermost part of a man's person to Heaven, and what pertains to Heaven, instead of being external to man, turns out to pertain to his truest nature. In a rather obscure passage, Mencius seems to be explaining just this point:

> The way the mouth is disposed towards tastes, the eye towards colours, the ear towards sounds, the nose towards smells, and the four limbs towards ease is human nature, yet therein also lies the Decree. That is why the gentleman does not describe it as nature. The way benevolence pertains to the relation between father and son, duty to the relation between prince and subject, the rites to the relation between guest and host, wisdom to the good and wise man, the sage to the way of Heaven, is the Decree, but therein also lies human nature. That is why the gentleman does not describe it as Decree. (VII. B. 24)

Mencius here begins by agreeing that it is human nature for a man's sense organs and other parts of the body to seek their respective objects for gratification, but what he emphatically denies is that one can be justified in acting immorally under the pretext that it is natural to pursue these ends. For the sphere of human action is also the sphere of morality, and we possess a heart which tells us whether we are doing right or not in our pursuit of this gratification. In his way of putting it, therein also lies the Decree. We know that in a conflict, human desires should give way to the Decree because we recognize the human heart as occupying a supreme position in the total nature of man. On the other hand, although there are moral duties arising from various human relationships, we must not describe them simply as Decreed. This is aimed at those who say that these duties may be decreed but it is just not possible to fulfil them. Mencius' point is that there are moral tendencies in human nature which in fact make it possible for man to fulfil these duties. Hence he says, 'therein also lies human nature'. There is one part of human nature which is one with Heaven. The other part which is not one with Heaven is merely that which we share with the animals. And this must not be allowed to stand in the way of a man's realizing his true nature. 'If one makes one's stand on what is of greater importance in the first instance, what is of smaller importance cannot displace it. In this way, one cannot but be a great man' (VI. A. 15).

In upholding the teachings of the Confucian tradition, Mencius was vigorous in combating what he considered heretical views. In particular, he was untiring in his attacks on the Schools of Yang Chu and Mo Ti. The latter persisted as a major school of thought well into the third century B.C., and it is not surprising that it formed one of Mencius' major targets. But the former was hardly a school to be reckoned with by the third century, and it is more difficult to understand why Mencius took it so seriously. It is likely that in the fourth century B.C. the school of Yang Chu was still of considerable influence, and, further, it may have been the precursor of the Taoist philosophers. Viewed in this light, Mencius was by no means mistaken in considering the teachings of Yang Chu as a major menace to the moral teachings of Confucius. Mencius chose a catch phrase from the teachings of each of the two figures for attention. In the case of Mo Tzu, it is the doctrine of love without discrimination (*chien ai*), while in the case of Yang Chu it is that of egoism (*wei wo*). Love without discrimination is indeed the backbone of Mo Tzu's teaching. According to this, a man should love all men equally without discrimination, and Mencius has not misrepresented it. He quotes a Mohist as saying, 'there should be no gradations in love' (III. A. 5). Egoism is equally the central doctrine of Yang Chu's teaching. According to Mencius, 'Yang Tzu chooses egoism. Even if he could benefit the Empire by pulling out one hair he would not do it' (VII. A. 26). In this Mencius is certainly guilty of misrepresentation. This is not quite the point of Yang Chu's egoism. It teaches that the most important possession a man has is his life, and the hedonists are mistaken in concluding that since a man lives only once he should indulge in as much pleasure as possible, for, in so doing, he runs the risk of wearing himself out before his time. Instead, a man should not do anything that can possibly harm his life. Hence in Yang Chu's view one should not give even one hair on one's body in exchange for the possession of the Empire. One hair, though insignificant, constitutes, nevertheless, part of one's body without which one cannot preserve one's life, and the possession of the Empire will almost certainly lead to over-indulgence in one's appetites. It is true that if one refused to give one hair in exchange for the possession of the Empire, *a fortiori* one would refuse to give a hair to benefit the Empire. Mencius' misrepresentation lies in taking what, properly speaking, is only a corollary and presenting it as the basic tenet of Yang Chu's teaching. But this makes no difference to the point of his criticism. His criticism is that 'Yang advocates everyone for himself, which amounts to a denial of one's prince' (III. B. 9). In other words, Yang opted out of his moral obligations to society, obligations that can only be met by taking part in public affairs. Yang's refusal to do so amounts to a 'denial of his prince'. On the other hand, love without discrimination advocated by Mo is a violation of the basic teaching of the Confucian school. One should treat one's fellow human beings with benevolence, but benevolence is based on the love one feels for one's parents: 'The content of benevolence is the serving of one's parents'' (IV. A. 27). It is by extending this love to others that one becomes a benevolent man. 'A benevolent man extends his love from those he loves to those he does not love' (VII. B. 1). 'There is just one thing in which the ancients greatly surpassed others, and that is the way they extended what they did' (I. A. 7). As benevolence is an extension of the natural love for one's parents to humanity at large through various degrees of kinship, it would be, according to Confucianists, unnatural to love all men alike. One should love one's parents more than other members of the family, other members of the family more than members of the same village and so on until one reaches humanity at large. Thus to love all men alike is to deny the claim of one's parents to a greater degree of love. Hence Mencius' description of the doctrine of love without discrimination as 'a denial of one's parents'.

Mencius concentrated all his attack on Yang and Mo, paying little attention to his contemporaries. The only group that come in for a certain amount of stricture are those whose teachings are aimed merely at strengthening the state politically and economically without a concomitant improvement in morality.

> Those who are in the service of princes today all say, 'I am able to extend the territory of my prince, and fill his coffers for him.' The good subject of today would have been looked upon in antiquity as a pest on the people. To enrich a prince who is neither attracted to the Way nor bent upon benevolence is to enrich a Chieh.
>
> Again, they say, 'I am able to gain allies and ensure victory in war for my prince.' The good subjects of today would have been looked upon in antiquity as a pest on the people. To try to make a prince strong in war who is neither attracted to the Way nor bent upon benevolence is to aid a Chieh. (VI. B. 9)

This is not very different from the criticism made by Confucius of one of his disciples quoted by Mencius with approval:

> While he was steward to the Chi family, Jan Ch'iu doubled the yield of taxation without being able to improve their virtue. Confucius said, 'Ch'iu is no disciple of mine. You, my young friends, may attack him to the beating of drums.' (VI. A. 14)

Mencius goes on to comment:

> From this it can be seen that Confucius rejected those who enriched rulers not given to the practice of benevolent government. How much more would he reject those who do their best to wage war on their behalf. In wars to gain land, the dead fill the plains; in wars to gain cities, the dead fill the cities. This is known as showing the land the way to devour human flesh. Death is too light a punishment for such men. Hence those skilled in war should suffer the most severe punishments; those who secure alliances with other feudal lords come next, and then come those who open up waste lands and increase the yield of the soil.

No doubt Mencius had such reformers as Wu Ch'i and Lord Shang, and scheming politicians like Chang Yi in mind, and his condemnation of them is in no uncertain terms.

On the whole Mencius rarely refers to his contemporaries. During the time he was in Ch'i, Chi Hsia was a great intellectual centre where a number of great thinkers forgathered, yet only two of them—Sung K'eng and Ch'un-yü K'un —are mentioned in the *Mencius* by name. One may, therefore, easily get the impression that Mencius was not conversant with the new ideas current in his time. But this is not altogether justified. Sometimes from the ideas he put forward we can see that he was familiar with what was going on around him. For instance, we have seen this to be the case with his 'flood like *ch'i*'. Again, sometimes from a turn of phrase he used we can also see the connexion with philosophical problems of the time. An interesting example is what he said when a meeting with Duke P'ing of Lu fell through. 'When a man goes forward,' said he, 'there is something which urges him on; when he halts, there is some-thing which holds him back. It is not in his power either to go forward or to halt. It is due to Heaven that I failed to meet the Marquis of Lu' (I. B. 16). The sentence 'When a man goes forward, there is something which urges him on' is a translation of *hsing huo shih chih* in which *huo shih chih* literally means 'something causes it'. Chapter 25 of the *Chuang tzu* mentions two theories, Chi Chen's theory of 'nothing does it (*mo wei*)' and Chieh Tzu's theory that 'something causes [it]'. Now we do not know who Chi Chen and Chieh Tzu were, but there is no doubt that these were cosmological theories, according to one of which there is nothing behind the universe while according to the other there is something that causes it to function. That the same phrase *huo shih* (or *huo chih shih*)[8] is used in the *Chuang tzu* shows that the *Mencius* and the *Chuang tzu* are talking about the same thing. Not only is Mencius on the side of there being 'something which causes it', but his further remark shows that this is what he understands by Heaven.

There is one other matter where Mencius shows himself to be conversant with current practice and that is the method of argument he uses. This is of considerable importance to a correct understanding of the *Mencius*. It is not uncommon for a reader of the *Mencius* to get the impression that Mencius was illogical and was unscrupulous towards his opponents. Arthur Waley, for instance, writes about Mencius as a disputant in the following vein:

As a controversialist he is nugatory. The whole discussion (Book VI) about whether Goodness and Duty are internal or external is a mass of irrelevant analogies, most of which could equally well be used to dis-prove what they are intended to prove. In other passages, the analogy gets mixed up with the actual point at issue. A glaring example is the discussion (IV. 1. XVII) with Shun-yü [this should be Ch'un-yü] K'un, who was shocked by Mencius's reluctance to take office. Shun-yü K'un's

---

[8] *Huo chih shih* in the *Chuang tzu* (8.31a-31b) is the same as *huo shih chih* in the *Mencius* except that in the former phrase the object *chih* is inverted.

argument is as follows: just as in a case of great urgency (despite the taboo on men and women touching hands) a man will give his hand to his sister-in-law to save her from drowning, so in the present emergency of China you ought to put aside the general principles that make you hesitate to take office, and place yourself at the disposal of the government. Mencius's reply is: 'When the world is drowning, it can only be rescued by the Way (of the Former Kings); when a sister-in-law is drowning, she can be rescued with the hand. Do you want me to rescue the world with my hand?'

This is at best a very cheap debating point. The proper answer (which may or may not have been made, but does not occur in *Mencius*) of course is, 'Figuratively yes. Just as one breaks taboos in an emergency and gives a hand to someone in peril, so I want you in the present political emergency to sacrifice your principles and "give a hand" to public affairs.'[9]

When language as intemperate as this is used of a philosopher, we naturally suspect that there must be a failure of understanding on the part of the critic, but when the philosopher in question happens to be one of the greatest in the ancient period of China, the suspicion cannot easily be dismissed.

The method of argument in common use in the fourth and third centuries B.C. in China is quite different from what we are used to. It consists of the use of analogy. This covers both the use of one thing to throw light on another and the use of one proposition we know to be true to throw light on another of similar form. It is fortunate for us that one of the chapters in the *Mo tzu* gives an account of this method of argument.[10] In using this method one starts with two propositions (1) and (2) which are similar in form and in being true. We argue that as we can derive another proposition (1.1) from (1) which is also true, we can similarly derive a true proposition (2.1) from (2). The *Mo tzu* criticizes this method by showing that it does not always hold. Let us take an example from the *Mo tzu*. We start with a pair of propositions:

(1) This horse's eyes are blind
(2) This horse's eyes are big.

They are identical in form, and let us assume that they are both true. Let us derive two propositions from them:

(1.1) This horse is blind.
(1.2) This horse is big.

[9] Arthur Waley, *Three Ways of Thought in Ancient China*, London, 1939, pp. 194-5. For an analysis of the arguments mentioned by Waley, see Appendix 5.

[10] For a discussion of this see D. C. Lau, 'Some Logical Problems in Ancient China' (*Proceedings of the Aristotelian Society*, Vol. LIII, 1952-3, pp. 189-204).

These are not only similar in form, but bear the same relationship to the original propositions. But we are mistaken if we think that, as the truth of (1.1) follows from that of (1), the truth of (2.1) must also follow from (2). As can be seen, it *follows* from 'this horse's eyes are blind' that 'this horse is blind', but it *does not follow* from 'this horse's eyes are big' that 'this horse is big'.

This is in fact the way analogies work. If we wish to throw light on something which is obscure, we make an analogy with some thing which is clear. Then we try to see whether because we can say something of the latter it follows that we can say something similar of the former. As analogues are rarely perfect, the analogy breaks down sooner or later. There are two points to bear in mind. First, an analogy is at least as instructive, if not more, when it breaks down as when it holds. Second, with subject matter that is obscure, intangible or elusive, analogy is often the only possible tool for probing its nature. And it is by this method that Mencius and his opponents grappled with philosophical problems. As both sides understood the method used, Mencius must have made more impression on his opponents than on the modern reader.

Let us take an example. In VI. A. 3, Kao Tzu begins with the statement

(1) That which is inborn (*sheng*) is what is meant by 'nature (*hsing*)'

and Mencius asks, 'Is that the same as

(2) White is what is meant by "white"?'

Kao Tzu said, 'Yes'.

Now we have good reason to believe that *sheng* (that which is inborn) and *hsing* (nature), being cognate words, were most probably written by the same character in Mencius' time, though they had, in all probability, a slightly different pronunciation. Thus both (1) and (2) are tautologous as written statements and also of exactly the same form.

Having elicited an assent from Kao Tzu, Mencius goes on to produce the proposition

(2.1) The whiteness of white feathers is the same as the whiteness of white snow and the whiteness of white snow is the same as the whiteness of white jade

and Kao Tzu agrees that this is a true proposition.

Then Mencius produces the further proposition

(1.1) The nature of a hound is the same as the nature of an ox and the nature of an ox is the same as the nature of a man.

The silence of Kao Tzu can only be taken to mean that even he was unable to accept this as true.

As the truth of (1.1) does not follow from the truth of (1) while the truth of (2.1) follows from that of (2), though (1.1) and (2.1) are similar in form and (1.1) bears the same relationship to (1) as (2.1) to (2), we can only conclude that 'white is what is meant by "white" ' is not a true analogue of 'that which is inborn is what is meant by "nature" ', and does not throw any light on it. This is the purpose of Mencius' argument and as this purpose is served, the argument is not taken any further—at least no further stage of the argument is recorded.

If we are interested in the grounds of the argument, we can analyse the two initial propositions and show that they are essentially different. The term 'nature' is a formal, empty term. The expression 'the nature of x' is not informative until x is specified. On the other hand, the term 'white' is not a formal, empty term but a term with a minimum specific content, so that the expression 'the whiteness of x' is informative even when x is not specified. To put it in another way, in the expression 'the nature of x', the term 'nature' is a function of x, while the term 'whiteness' in the expression 'the whiteness of x' is not a function of x.

The difference also comes out in another way. We may notice that in the expression 'the whiteness of white feathers', the term 'white' is repeated before 'feathers', while there is no such repetition in the expression 'the nature of a dog'. This is because 'whiteness' is a contingent character of 'feathers' whereas 'the nature' of a dog is not a contingent character of the dog.

By saying that 'that which is inborn is "nature" ', Kao Tzu no doubt meant to say that 'nature is nature' whether it is the nature of an animal or a man. This is connected with his view that 'appetite for food and sex is nature'. If by this is meant simply that appetites are what man has in common with animals, then Mencius would have no quarrel with it, but it is easy to take 'nature is nature' to mean that there is total identity of nature between man and animals. And we have seen that, when this implication was brought out into the open, not even Kao Tzu was willing to go so far as to accept it. If Kao Tzu admits that only part of the nature of man is identical with the nature of animals, then the question would centre on the significance of the distinctively human part of a man's nature. This takes Kao Tzu and Mencius beyond the immediate concern which is the precise implications of the statement 'that which is inborn is "nature" '. The only point established is that the statement 'white is what is meant by "white" ' throws no light on the problem as the similarity in form between the two statements is more apparent than real.[11]

[11] For an analysis of further examples of Mencius' arguments, see   D. C. Lau, 'On

Let us turn to Mencius' political philosophy. This is not only consistent with his moral philosophy but is derived from it. Ancient Chinese thinkers all looked upon politics as a branch of morals. More precisely, the relationship between the ruler and the subject was looked upon as a special case of the moral relationship which holds between individuals. Like his moral theory, Mencius' political theory rests on the concept of Heaven. First, Mencius has absolutely no doubt that the ruler is set up by Heaven for the benefit of the people. Hence whether a ruler deserves to remain a ruler depends on whether he carries out his duty or not. If he does not, he should be removed. In a justly celebrated passage, Mencius says:

> The people are of supreme importance; the altars to the gods of earth and grain come next; last comes the ruler.

He goes on to develop this in these words:

> When a feudal lord endangers the altars to the gods of earth and grain he should be replaced. When the sacrificial animals are sleek, the offerings are clean and the sacrifices are observed at due times, and yet floods and droughts come, then the altars should be replaced. (VII. B. 14)

In other words, if a ruler endangers the independence of the state—of which the altars to the gods of earth and grain are the symbol—and so endangers the people, he ought to be replaced. And even the gods of earth and grain are not above replacement if, in spite of the fact that sacrifices are duly offered to them, they fail to prevent floods and droughts which harm the people. Thus we can see the full significance of the supremacy of the people.

The removal of the ruler is a subject Mencius touches upon on more than one occasion. When asked about ministers by King Hsüan of Ch'i, Mencius said that ministers of royal blood would not hesitate to depose a ruler who refused repeatedly to listen to admonitions against serious mistakes (V. B. 9). Again, when asked whether it was justified for a good subject to banish a bad ruler, Mencius answered that provided that one had the lofty motives of a Yi Yin it was justified (VII. A. 31). As we can see from this example, the term 'ruler' covers the Emperor as well as rulers of feudal states. In fact the classic examples of the deposition of evil rulers are to be found in the transition of the Three Dynasties. Chieh, the last Emperor of the Hsia Dynasty, and Tchou, the last Emperor of the Shang (or Yin) Dynasty, are bywords for depravity. The former was deposed by T'ang, the founder of the Shang, and the latter by King Wu, the founder of the Chou, by military force. The attitude Mencius takes towards these historical examples is unambiguous:

Mencius' Use of the Method of Analogy in Argument' (*Asia Major*, Vol. X, 1963, pp. 173-94), reprinted in Appendix 5.

King Hsüan of Ch'i asked, 'Is it true that T'ang banished Chieh and King Wu marched against Tchou?'

'It is so recorded,' answered Mencius.

'Is regicide permissible?'

'He who mutilates benevolence is a multilator; he who cripples rightness is a crippler; and a man who is both a mutilator and a crippler is an "outcast". I have indeed heard of the punishment of the "outcast Tchou", but I have not heard of any regicide.' (I. B. 8)

For Mencius a man who is a mutilator of benevolence and a crippler of rightness is an outcast. That he happens to be an emperor makes no difference. Indeed it makes the situation worse. 'Only the benevolent man is fit to be in high position. For a cruel man to be in high position is for him to disseminate his wickedness among the people' (IV. A. 1). And there is no higher position than that of Emperor.

On one occasion in the Western Han, the question whether in deposing Chieh and Tchou, T'ang and King Wu received the Mandate of Heaven was debated by two scholars, Yüan-ku Sheng and Huang Sheng, before Emperor Ching (reigned 156-141 B.C.). The former, echoing Mencius' view, said, 'Chieh and Tchou were cruel and disorderly, and the heart of the Empire turned towards T'ang and King Wu who, following the wishes of the Empire, punished Chieh and Tchou. As the people of the Empire no longer obeyed Chieh and Tchou and turned to T'ang and King Wu, they had no alternative but to ascend the throne. If this is not receiving the Mandate, what is?' Huang Sheng, on the other hand, retorted by saying, 'A hat, however well-worn, should only be put on the head, while a shoe, however new, should only be put on the foot. This is because there is a distinction between "above" and "below". Now though Chieh and Tchou no longer followed the Way, they were, nevertheless, rulers above, while T'ang and King Wu, though they were sages, were, nevertheless, subjects below. When an Emperor does anything wrong, and a subject, instead of putting him right by proper advice to safeguard the dignity of the office, puts himself on the throne instead, what is this, if not regicide?' When Yüan-ku cited the example of the overthrow of the Ch'in by the first Emperor of the Han, the debate threatened to get out of hand, and Emperor Ching had to step in with the famous words, 'It is no reflection on one's discerning palate if, in eating meat, one does not wish to try horse's liver. It is no reflection on one's intelligence if, in one's discussion, one keeps off the subject of whether T'ang and King Wu received the Mandate of Heaven'[12]

Though the unbroken tradition of autocratic rule in China effectively killed Mencius' theory of the right of the people to depose an oppressive ruler,

---

[12] See *Shih chi*, chüan 121, *Han shu*, chüan 88.

the less radical part of his theory that the Emperor existed for the sake of the people and not the other way round has never been questioned.

Yüan-ku Sheng's view is, indeed, an accurate statement of Mencius' position. In singling out 'the heart of the Empire' he has hit upon its central doctrine. As Mencius puts it,

> It was through losing the people that Chieh and Tchou lost the Empire, and through losing the people's hearts that they lost the people. There is a way to win the Empire; win the people and you will win the Empire. There is a way to win the people; win their hearts and you will win the people. (IV. A. 9)

The emphasis on the heart is firmly based on Mencius' moral theory. First, the heart is endowed with the ability to judge between right and wrong, and as the relationship between ruler and subject is simply one instance of moral relationship, political action on the part of the ruler is as much subject to moral judgement as any other kind of action. Second, as we have seen, the human heart constitutes a bridge linking man with Heaven, and there is no more infallible indication of the will of Heaven than the reaction to the ruler of the people in their hearts. This problem about the will of Heaven was raised when Wan Chang asked Mencius how Heaven was supposed to have given the Empire to Shun. Did Heaven give detailed and minute instructions to him? No. Heaven did not speak but revealed itself through its acts and deeds. As the *T'ai shih* had it, Heaven sees with the eyes of its people; Heaven hears with the ears of its people (V. A. 5). Behind this talk about Heaven, there is a firm conviction on Mencius' part that it is impossible, in the long run, for a ruler to take the people in. If he governs with their welfare at heart, they will know it, but if he only pretends to do so, they will see through it. In other words, reduced to its fundamentals, moral judgement is something well within the capability of even the most simple-minded. This is a belief shared by most moral thinkers of the world, of whatever time and place, because it is, in fact, a *sine qua non* of the possibility of morality at all.

What is the welfare of the people? This is a question to which there is a simple answer. The most basic need of the people is a reasonable and steady livelihood. A man must be able to support all his family, his parents on the one hand, and his wife and children on the other. With this end in view, a man must not be taken away from productive work during busy seasons. Corvée duties should be kept within manageable limits and to the off seasons. A ruler, in Mencius' view, is sure to act correctly if he has the right attitude to his people. He should be both father and mother to them. We can see, once again, that the relationship between ruler and subject is looked upon as resting on a personal and moral basis. We can also see why, for Mencius, the characteristic virtue of the ruler is benevolence, for benevolence is exemplified by the love between parent and child. 'The content of benevolence is the serving of one's parents' (IV. A. 27). 'Loving one's parents is benevolence' (VII. A. 15). The motive behind benevolence is the love between parent and child, and the ruler must feel something of this love for his people before he can become a good ruler. As we have seen, the love a ruler feels for his people is not identical with, but an extension of, the love felt by a parent for his child. This is clearly stated by Mencius in a number of places. For instances, 'A gentleman . . . shows benevolence towards the people but is not attached to them. He is attached to his parents but is merely benevolent towards the people' (VII. A. 45). The mistake of the Mohist, in the eyes of the Confucianist, is that he 'believes that a man loves his brother's son no more than his neighbour's newborn babe'[13] (III. A. 5). For the Confucianist, it is natural for a man to love his parent or son, and it is only through pushing this outwards stage by stage that he succeeds in loving all humanity. But as the love for humanity is only an extension of the love for parent or son, it is only natural that one's fellow human beings have less claim on one than one's parent or son.

Thus Mencius' ideal of a state can be summed up by the term 'benevolent government'. So long as the ruler is motivated by benevolence, the people will understand and accept whatever measure he finds it necessary to take. 'If the services of the people were used with a view to sparing them hardship, they would not complain even when hard driven. If people were put to death in pursuance of a policy to keep them alive, they would die bearing no ill-will towards the man who put them to death' (VII. A. 12).

We have already pointed out that for Confucius benevolence was the totality of the moral qualities in man. For Mencius, benevolence was more specifically the virtue that characterizes the relationship between parent and child. By extension, it was the virtue typical of the ruler. The difference between the way Confucius used the term and the way Mencius used it can be seen from the fact that the expression 'benevolent government' which forms the cornerstone of Mencius' political philosophy is not to be found at all in the *Analects of Confucius*.

As Mencius believed that the ruler existed for the sake of the people, he had to justify his objection to the proposal by more radical thinkers that the ruler should work side by side with his people in order to justify his existence. Mencius pointed out that for society to function at all there must be people engaged in different kinds of work. A farmer is certainly a man who works for his living, but even a farmer cannot do his own work and, at the same

---

[13] Cf. 'My brother I love, but the brother of a man from Ch'in I do not love.' (VI. A. 4)

time, engage in making the hundred and one things needed in his daily life. He has to trade the surplus of his produce for the fruits of other people's labour. Why, then, should this not apply to the ruler? The work of government is a good deal more arduous than working in the fields. Why should one expect the ruler to be able to produce his own food and carry on the work of government at the same time?

This may justify the ruler's not working on the land, but the question remains, why should he enjoy a life far above that of the common people in luxury and comfort? The answer is twofold. First, the work of government is so much more important. Any incompetence on the part of the ruler will affect the whole state while an incompetent farmer will ruin only his own plot. Second, the ruler uses his heart, or, as we should say, his mind, while the common man uses his muscles, and it is natural for the latter to be ruled by the former. Here we can see that, for Mencius, the pattern of the body politic is similar to the pattern of the human body. A man's body consists of many parts, and, as we have seen, the importance of the heart as an organ is far greater than that of any other part of the body. It is the master of the whole body. Similarly, the ruler in the body politic is supreme. One can go even further and say that the supreme position of the ruler in the body politic is derived from the fact that the heart is supreme in the body; he uses his heart while the common man uses only his muscles. This is supported by Mencius' use of the terms 'great' and 'small'. As we have seen, according to Mencius the parts of the body vary in importance. Some are of 'greater' importance and some are of 'smaller' importance. He who nurtures the parts of smaller importance is a small man; he who nurtures the parts of greater importance is a great man (VI. A. 14). Again, Mencius says, 'One who is guided by the interests of the parts of his person that are of greater importance is a great man; one who is guided by the interests of the parts of his person that are of smaller importance is a small man. (VI. A. 15). The part of greatest importance is of course the heart. So a man who puts his heart first is a great man, and a man who puts his limbs first is a small man. It cannot be a coincidence that, in describing the distinction between the ruler and the ruled, Mencius uses the same terms. 'There are affairs of great men and there are affairs of small men' (III. A. 4). That the terms are used in the same way is confirmed by the fact that the great men who rule exercise their hearts, while the small men who are ruled exercise their muscles. If this conclusion is correct, then we can say that the pattern of the body politic is not only similar to the pattern of the body but is in fact a projection of it.

Mencius' attitude towards war follows logically from his belief in the supremacy of the people. War brings great suffering to the people as they are the ones who get killed and it is their land that is laid waste. Hence it is

xxxviii   Introduction

something to be abhorred, and should be resorted to only as a desperate remedy. There are two conditions which must be fulfilled before war can be justified. First, it should be used to remove wicked rulers who cannot be removed by any other means. Second, even when directed towards this end, war should only be initiated by someone who has the authority. When these two conditions are fulfilled, the result is what Mencius would call a punitive war. Again, we can see the moral basis of what is political. War is to a state —and so to the ruler—what punishment is to the criminal. When questioned whether he encouraged Ch'i to invade Yen, Mencius replied that he did not. All he did was to say that Yen deserved invasion. As Ch'i was no better than Yen, there was no moral justification for the invasion. In other words, Ch'i had not the moral authority. Only a Heaven-appointed officer had the authority to do so, just as only the Marshal of the Guards had the authority to put a murderer to death (II. B. 8). Elsewhere Mencius says that when the ruler of a state is looked up to even by the people in neighbouring states as their father and mother, he will have no match in the Empire. And he who has no match in the Empire is a Heaven-appointed officer (II. A. 5). So the Heaven-appointed officer turns out to be the ruler who practises benevolent government.

No war other than punitive wars are justified. 'The *Spring and Autumn Annals* acknowledge no just wars,' said Mencius. 'There are only cases of one war not being quite as bad as another. A punitive expedition is a war waged by one in authority against his subordinates. It is not for peers to punish one another by war' (VII. B. 2).

Together with war, Mencius condemned those who were experts at waging war. 'Those skilled in war should suffer the most severe punishment.' For in war enough men are killed to fill the plains and cities which are in dispute. 'This is known as showing the land the way to devour human flesh. Death is too light a punishment' for men 'who do their best to wage war for a prince' (IV. A. 14). If a ruler is benevolent he will have no match in the Empire (VII. B. 4), but if a prince is not benevolent, to extend his territory for him is to be a pest on the people (VI. B. 9). As we have seen, this condemnation is not confined to waging war for the prince. Simply to enrich a prince who is not benevolent is to be a pest on the people.

Let us try to sum up the contributions made by Mencius to Confucian thought. With the passage of time, new developments and new problems arose, and if Confucianism was to hold its own, it had to take cognizance of these new developments and furnish answers to these new problems. First, the problem of human nature which hardly existed in Confucius' day became a hotly debated issue. There were a number of different views. According to some, human nature is neutral: human beings can be made good or bad. According to others, there is neither good nor bad in human nature. According to others again, human nature consists solely of appetites and desires. What Mencius did was to offer his own theory which is not only consistent with, but can furnish a firm basis to, Confucian thought. This is his theory that human nature is good.

Second, the fourth century B.C. can be looked upon as a watershed in the history of Chinese thought in the ancient period. It marks the discovery of the human heart or mind. In the *Analects of Confucius* and the parts of the *Mo tzu* which are earliest in date, although the heart (*hsin*) is actually mentioned, there is no reference to its inner complexities. But by the middle of the fourth century B.C., at the latest, philosophers discovered the complex phenomenon of the human heart and became fascinated by it. This, as we have seen, was initially connected with the theory that *ch'i* was the basic ingredient in the universe. Again, Mencius not only took cognizance of what happened but also produced his own distinctive way of looking at the matter. He produced a moral version of the theory of the heart and *ch'i*.

Finally, in the fourth century B.C. the question was discussed whether there was something behind the universe without which it would cease to function. We have seen that of the two opposing views, 'nothing does it' and 'something causes it', Mencius definitely ranged himself on the side of the second, and this he identified with the earlier belief in Heaven and so related it to the problem of the Mandate or Decree of Heaven.

Mencius brought all these threads together into a complex system. The unique feature of the make-up of a human being is his heart, and so when we speak of human nature we should have in mind, primarily, the human heart. This heart contains incipient moral tendencies which when nurtured with care can enable a man to become a sage. As it is Heaven which is responsible for making morality the unique distinguishing feature of man, his moral nature is that which links him with Heaven. The flood-like *ch'i* which is a manifestation of this nature, when developed to the utmost, fills the space between Heaven and Earth, and when that happens Man is in the same stream as Heaven and Earth. Thus the barrier between the Decree of Heaven and the Nature of Man which some saw as insuperable was shown by Mencius to be non-existent, and there was no obstacle in man's path to a perfect moral character except his own failure to make the effort.

It is a view commonly accepted that the Taoist philosophers Lao Tzu and Chuang Tzu represented mysticism in ancient China. In my view, the *Tao te ching*, which is supposed to have been written by Lao Tzu, contains ideas that are down-to-earth rather than mystic, as the aim was to help a man pick his way through all the hazards inherent in living in a disorderly age. Chuang Tzu, on the other hand, has a better claim to being a mystic. He had a vision of a universe that transcended values which are, at best, of only limited validity. The purpose of his view of the universe is to foster an attitude of resignation. There was, for Chuang Tzu, no safe recipe for survival. The only thing a man can do is to refuse to recognize the conventional values assigned to life and death. In Chuang Tzu's thought there is a sense of oneness with the universe, and that is what qualifies him as a mystic, but a true mystic, it seems to me, ought to feel that the universe has a purpose and this is missing in Chuang Tzu. Mencius, on the other hand, is more truly a mystic. Not only does he believe that a man can attain oneness with the universe by perfecting his own moral nature, but he has absolute faith in the moral purpose of the universe. His great achievement is that he not only successfully defended the teachings of Confucius against the corrosive influence of new ideas but, in the process, added to Confucianism a depth that it did not possess before.

D. C. L.

MENCIUS 孟子

梁惠王章句上

1.　孟子見梁惠王。王曰:"叟!不遠千里而來,亦將有以利吾國乎?"

　　孟子對曰:"王!何必曰利?亦有仁義而已矣。王曰,'何以利吾國?'大夫曰,'何以利吾家?'士庶人曰,'何以利吾身?'上下交征利而國危矣。萬乘之國,弒其君者,必千乘之家;千乘之國,弒其君者,必百乘之家。萬取千焉,千取百焉,不爲不多矣。苟爲後義而先利,不奪不饜。未有仁而遺其親者也,未有義而後其君者也。王亦曰,'仁義而已矣,何必曰利?'"

2.　孟子見梁惠王。王立於沼上,顧鴻鴈麋鹿,曰:"賢者亦樂此乎?"

　　孟子對曰:"賢者而後樂此,不賢者雖有此不樂也。詩云:'經始靈臺,經之營之,庶民攻之,不日成之。經始勿亟,庶民子來。王在靈囿,麀鹿攸伏,麀鹿濯濯,白鳥鶴鶴。王在靈沼,於牣魚躍。'文王以民力爲臺爲沼,而民歡樂之,謂其臺曰靈臺,謂其沼曰靈沼,樂其有麋鹿魚鼈。古之人與民偕樂,故能樂也。湯誓曰:'時日害喪,予及女偕亡。'民欲與之偕亡,雖有臺池鳥獸,豈能獨樂哉?"

BOOK I · PART A

1. Mencius went to see King Hui of Liang. 'Sir,' said the King. 'You have come all this distance, thinking nothing of a thousand *li*.[1] You must surely have some way of profiting my state?'

'Your Majesty,' answered Mencius. 'What is the point of mentioning the word "profit"? All that matters is that there should be benevolence and rightness. If Your Majesty says, "How can I profit my state?" and the Counsellors say, "How can I profit my family?" and the Gentlemen[2] and Commoners say, "How can I profit my person?" then those above and those below will be trying to profit at the expense of one another and the state will be imperilled. When regicide is committed in a state of ten thousand chariots, it is certain to be by a vassal with a thousand chariots, and when it is committed in a state of a thousand chariots, it is certain to be by a vassal with a hundred chariots. A share of a thousand in ten thousand or a hundred in a thousand is by no means insignificant, yet if profit is put before rightness, there is no satisfaction short of total usurpation. No benevolent man ever abandons his parents, and no dutiful man ever puts his prince last. Perhaps you will now endorse what I have said, "All that matters is that there should be benevolence and rightness. What is the point of mentioning the word 'profit'?" '

[1] A little over 400 metres.

[2] In the present translation, 'Gentleman' is used to translate *shih* while 'gentleman' is used to translate *chün tzu*. *Shih* was the lowest rank of officials while *chün tzu* denoted either a man of moral excellence or a man in authority. The decision to use the same word for translating both these Chinese terms is not entirely arbitrary, as *shih chün tzu* is a term commonly used in the *Mo tzu* and the *Hsün tzu*.

2. Mencius went to see King Hui of Liang. The King was standing over a pond. 'Are such things enjoyed even by a good and wise man?' said he, looking round at his wild geese and deer.

'Only if a man is good and wise,' answered Mencius, 'is he able to enjoy them. Otherwise he would not, even if he had them.

'The *Odes* say,

> He surveyed and began the Sacred Terrace.
> He surveyed it and measured it;

3. 梁惠王曰："寡人之於國也，盡心焉耳矣。河內凶，則移其民於河東，移其粟於河內。河東凶亦然。察鄰國之政，無如寡人之用心者。鄰國之民不加少，寡人之民不加多，何也？"

孟子對曰："王好戰，請以戰喻。塡然鼓之，兵刃既接，棄甲曳兵而走。或百步而後止，或五十步而後止。以五十步笑百步，則何如？"

曰："不可；直不百步耳，是亦走也。"

曰："王如知此，則無望民之多於鄰國也。

> The people worked at it;
> In less than no time they finished it.
> He surveyed and began without haste;
> The people came in ever increasing numbers.
> The King was in the Sacred Park.
> The doe lay down;
> The doe were sleek;
> The white birds glistened.
> The King was at the Sacred Pond.
> Oh! how full it was of leaping fish![3]

It was with the labour of the people that King Wen built his terrace and pond, yet so pleased and delighted were they that they named his terrace the "Sacred Terrace" and his pond the "Sacred Pond", and rejoiced in his possession of deer, fish and turtles. It was by sharing their enjoyments with the people that men of antiquity were able to enjoy themselves.

'The *T'ang shih* says,

> O Sun,[4] when wilt thou perish?
> We care not if we have to die with thee.[5]

When the people were prepared "to die with" him, even if the tyrant had a terrace and pond, birds and beasts, could he have enjoyed them all by himself?'

[3] Ode 242.

[4] The Sun stands for the tyrant Chieh whom the people did not dare name openly. Chieh was said to have remarked, 'My possession of the Empire is like there being a sun in Heaven. Is there a time when the sun will perish? If the sun perishes, then I shall perish.' (*Han shih wai chuan*, 2/22).

[5] See *Shu ching*, 8.2b.

3. King Hui of Liang said, 'I have done my best for my state. When crops failed in Ho Nei I moved the population to Ho Tung and the grain to Ho Nei, and reversed the action when crops failed in Ho Tung. I have not noticed any of my neighbours taking as much pains over his government. Yet how is it the population of the neighbouring states has not decreased and mine has not increased?'

'Your Majesty is fond of war,' said Mencius. May I use an analogy from it? After weapons were crossed to the rolling of drums, some soldiers fled, abandoning their armour and trailing

　　“不違農時，穀不可勝食也；數罟不入洿池，魚鼈不可勝食也；斧斤以時入山林，材木不可勝用也。穀與魚鼈不可勝食，材木不可勝用，是使民養生喪死無憾也。養生喪死無憾，王道之始也。

　　“五畝之宅，樹之以桑，五十者可以衣帛矣。雞豚狗彘之畜，無失其時，七十者可以食肉矣。百畝之田，勿奪其時，數口之家可以無飢矣。謹庠序之教，申之以孝悌之義，頒白者不負戴於道路矣。七十者衣帛食肉，黎民不飢不寒，然而不王者，未之有也。

　　“狗彘食人食而不知檢，塗有餓莩而不知發；人死，則曰，‘非我也，歲也。’是何異於刺人而殺之，曰，‘非我也，兵也。’王無罪歲，斯天下之民至焉。”

their weapons. One stopped after a hundred paces, another after fifty paces. What would you think if the latter, as one who ran only fifty paces, were to laugh at the former who ran a hundred?'

'He had no right to,' said the King. 'He did not quite run a hundred paces. That is all. But all the same, he ran.'

'If you can see that,' said Mencius, 'you will not expect your own state to be more populous than the neighbouring states.

'If you do not interfere with the busy seasons in the fields, then there will be more grain than the people can eat; if you do not allow nets with too fine a mesh to be used in large ponds, then there will be more fish and turtles than they can eat; if hatchets and axes are permitted in the forests on the hills only in the proper seasons, then there will be more timber than they can use. When the people have more grain, more fish and turtles than they can eat, and more timber than they can use, then in the support of their parents when alive and in the mourning of them when dead, they will be able to have no regrets over anything left undone.[6] For the people not to have any regrets over anything left undone, whether in the support of their parents when alive or in the mourning of them when dead is the first step along the Kingly way.

'If the mulberry is planted in every homestead of five *mu*[7] of land, then those who are fifty can wear silk; if chickens, pigs and dogs do not miss their breeding season, then those who are seventy can eat meat; if each lot of a hundred *mu* is not deprived of labour during the busy seasons, then families with several mouths to feed will not go hungry. Exercise due care over the education provided by the village schools, and discipline the people by teaching them the duties proper to sons and younger brothers, and those whose heads have turned hoary will not be carrying loads on the roads. When those who are seventy wear[8] silk and eat meat and the masses are neither cold nor hungry, it is impossible for their prince not to be a true King.

'Now when food meant for human beings is so plentiful as to be thrown to dogs and pigs, you fail to realize that it is time for collection, and when men drop dead from starvation by the way-side, you fail to realize that it is time for distribution. When people die, you simply say, "It is none of my doing. It is the fault of the harvest." In what way is that different from killing a man by

4.　梁惠王曰：“寡人願安承教。”

孟子對曰：“殺人以梃與刃，有以異乎？”

　　曰：“無以異也。”

　　“以刃與政，有以異乎？”

　　曰：“無以異也。”

　　曰：“庖有肥肉，廄有肥馬，民有飢色，野有餓莩，此率獸而食人也。獸相食，且人惡之；為民父母，行政，不免於率獸而食人，惡在其為民父母也？仲尼曰：‘始作俑者，其無後乎！’為其象人而用之也。如之何其使斯民飢而死也？”

5.　梁惠王曰：“晉國，天下莫強焉，叟之所知也。及寡人之身，東敗於齊，長子死焉；西喪地於秦七百里；南辱於楚。寡人恥之，願比死者壹洒之，如之何則可？”

　　孟子對曰：“地方百里而可以王。王如施仁政於民，省刑罰，薄稅斂，深耕易耨；壯者以暇日修其孝悌忠信，入以事其父兄，出以事

running him through, while saying all the time, "Is it none of my doing. It is the fault of the weapon." Stop putting the blame on the harvest and the people of the whole Empire will come to you.'

[6]Presumably because they have no lack of food for the support of the living or of timber for coffins in which to bury the dead.

[7]As a *mu* is one nine-hundredth part of a square *li*, it works out to be somewhat less than 200 square metres.

[8]This passage is found again in I. A. 7 where, instead of 'those who are seventy', the text reads 'the aged' which seems preferable, as 'those who wear silk and eat meat' refers as much to those who are fifty as to those who are seventy.

4. King Hui of Liang said, 'I shall listen willingly to what you have to say.'[9]

'Is there any difference,' said Mencius, 'between killing a man with a staff and killing him with a knife?'

'There is no difference.'

'Is there any difference between killing him with a knife and killing him with misrule?'

'There is no difference.'

'There is fat meat in your kitchen and there are well-fed horses in your stables, yet the people look hungry and in the outskirts of cities men drop dead from starvation. This is to lead the animals in the devouring of men. Even the devouring of animals by animals is repugnant to men. If, then, one who is father and mother to the people cannot, in ruling over them, avoid leading animals in the devouring of men, wherein is he father and mother to the people?

'When Confucius said, "The inventor of burial figures in human form deserves not to have any progeny," he was condemning him for the use of something modelled after the human form. How, then, can the starving of this very people be countenanced?'

[9]In view of the opening remark, it is likely that this chapter forms a unity with the previous chapter.

5. King Hui of Liang said, 'As you know, the state of Chin[10] was second to none in power in the Empire. But when it came to my own time we suffered defeat in the east by Ch'i when my eldest son died, and we lost territory to the extent of seven hundred *li* to Ch'in in the west, while to the south we were humiliated by Ch'u. I am deeply ashamed of this and wish, in what little time I

其長上，可使制梃以撻秦楚之堅甲利兵矣。

"彼奪其民時，使不得耕耨以養其父母。父母凍餓，兄弟妻子離散。彼陷溺其民，王往而征之，夫誰與王敵？故曰：'仁者無敵。'王請勿疑！"

6. 　孟子見梁襄王，出，語人曰："望之不似人君，就之而不見所畏焉。卒然問曰：'天下惡乎定？'

"吾對曰：'定於一。'

"'孰能一之？'

"對曰：'不嗜殺人者能一之。'

"'孰能與之？'

"對曰：'天下莫不與也。王知夫苗乎？七八月之間旱，則苗槁矣。天油然作雲，沛然下雨，則苗浡然興之矣。其如是，孰能禦之？今夫天下之人牧，未有不嗜殺人者也。如有不嗜殺人者，則天下之民皆引領而望之矣。誠如是也，民歸之，由水之就下，沛然誰能禦之？'"

have left in this life, to wash away all this shame. How can this be done?'

'A territory of a hundred *li* square,' answered Mencius, 'is sufficient to enable its ruler to become a true King. If Your Majesty practises benevolent government towards the people, reduces punishment and taxation, gets the people to plough deeply and weed promptly, and if the able-bodied men learn, in their spare time, to be good sons and good younger brothers, loyal to their prince and true to their word, so that they will, in the family, serve their fathers and elder brothers, and outside the family, serve their elders and superiors, then they can be made to inflict defeat on the strong armour and sharp weapons of Ch'in and Ch'u, armed with nothing but staves.

'These other princes take the people away from their work during the busy .seasons, making it impossible for them to till the land and so minister to the needs of their parents. Thus parents suffer cold and hunger while brothers, wives and children are separated and scattered. These princes push their people into pits and into water. If you should go and punish such princes, who is there to oppose you? Hence it is said, "The benevolent man has no match." I beg of you not to have any doubts.'

[10] Men of Liang often referred to their own state as Chin.

6. Mencius saw King Hsiang of Liang. Coming away, he said to someone, 'When I saw him at a distance he did not look like a ruler of men and when I went close to him I did not see anything that commanded respect. Abruptly he asked me, "Through what can the Empire be settled?"

' "Through unity," I said.

' "Who can unite it?"

' "One who is not fond of killing can unite it," I said.

' "Who can give it to him?"[11]

' "No one in the Empire will refuse to give it to him. Does Your Majesty not know about the young seedling? Should there be a drought in the seventh or eighth month, it will wilt. If clouds begin to gather in the sky and rain comes pouring down, then it will spring up again. This being the case, who can stop it? Now in

7.　齊宣王問曰：“齊桓、晉文之事可得聞乎？”

　　孟子對曰：“仲尼之徒無道桓文之事者，是以後世無傳焉，臣未之聞也。無以則王乎？”

　　曰：“德何如則可以王矣？”

　　曰：“保民而王，莫之能禦也。”

　　曰：“若寡人者，可以保民乎哉？”

　　曰：“可。”

　　曰：“何由知吾可也？”

　　曰：“臣聞之胡齕曰，王坐於堂上，有牽牛而過堂下者，王見之，曰：‘牛何之？’對曰：‘將以釁鐘。’王曰：‘舍之！吾不忍其觳觫，若無罪而就死地。’對曰：‘然則廢釁鐘與？’曰：‘何可廢也？以羊易之！’——不識有諸？”

　　曰：“有之。”

　　曰：“是心足以王矣。百姓皆以王爲愛也，臣固知王之不忍也。”

the Empire amongst the shepherds of men there is not one who is
not fond of killing. If there is one who is not, then the people
in the Empire will crane their necks to watch for his coming. This
being truly the case, the people will turn to him like water flowing
downwards with a tremendous force. Who can stop it?" '

[11]For this idea of giving someone the Empire, cf. the sentence in V. A. 5, 6 'Who
gave it to him'. Cf. further 'Hence it is easy to give the Empire away but difficult to find
the right person for it' (III. A. 4), and 'Following the way of the present day, unless
there is a change in the ways of the people, a man could not hold the Empire for the dura-
tion of one morning, even if it were given him' (VI. B. 9). It is, however, possible that
the text is corrupt. For a suggested emendation see D. C. Lau, 'Some Notes on the
Mencius', *Asia Major* Vol. XV (1969), which is reprinted as Appendix 6.

7. King Hsüan of Ch'i asked, 'Can you tell me about the history of
Duke Huan of Ch'i and Duke Wen of Chin?'

'None of the followers of Confucius,' answered Mencius, 'spoke
of the history of Duke Huan and Duke Wen. It is for this reason
that no one in after ages passed on any accounts, and I have no
knowledge of them. If you insist, perhaps I may be permitted to
tell you about becoming a true King.'

'How virtuous must a man be before he can become a true
King?'

'He becomes a true King by tending the people. This is something no one can stop.'

'Can someone like myself tend the people?'

'Yes.'

'How do you know that I can?'

'I heard the following from Hu He:

The King was sitting in the hall. He saw someone passing below, leading an
ox. The King noticed this and said, "Where is the ox going?" "The blood of
the ox is to be used for consecrating a new bell." "Spare it. I cannot bear to
see it shrinking with fear, like an innocent man going to the place of execution." "In that case, should the ceremony be abandoned?" "That is out of
the question. Use a lamb instead."

' I wonder if this is true?'

'It is.'

'The heart behind your action is sufficient to enable you to
become a true King. The people all thought that you grudged the

王曰："然；誠有百姓者。齊國雖褊小，吾何愛一牛？即不忍其
觳觫，若無罪而就死地，故以羊易之也。"

曰："王無異於百姓之以王爲愛也。以小易大，彼惡知之？王若
隱其無罪而就死地，則牛羊何擇焉？"

王笑曰："是誠何心哉？我非愛其財，而易之以羊也。宜乎百姓
之謂我愛也。"

曰："無傷也，是乃仁術也，見牛未見羊也。君子之於禽獸也，
見其生，不忍見其死；聞其聲，不忍食其肉。是以君子遠庖廚也。"

王說曰："詩云：'他人有心，予忖度之。'夫子之謂也。夫我
乃行之，反而求之，不得吾心。夫子言之，於我心有戚戚焉。此心之
所以合於王者，何也？"

曰："有復於王者曰：'吾力足以舉百鈞，而不足以舉一羽；明
足以察秋毫之末，而不見輿薪，則王許之乎？"

曰："否。"

"今恩足以及禽獸，而功不至於百姓者，獨何與？然則一羽之不
舉，爲不用力焉；輿薪之不見，爲不用明焉；百姓之不見保，爲不用
恩焉。故王之不王，不爲也，非不能也。"

expense, but, for my part, I have no doubt that you were moved by pity for the animal.'

'You are right,' said the King. 'How extraordinary that there should be such people! Ch'i may be a small state, but I am not quite so miserly as to grudge the use of an ox. It was simply because I could not bear to see it shrink with fear, like an innocent man going to the place of execution, that I used a lamb instead.'

'You must not be surprised that the people thought you miserly. You used a small animal in place of a big one. How were they to know? If you were pained by the animal going innocently to its death, what was there to choose between an ox and a lamb?'

The King laughed and said, 'What was really in my mind, I wonder? It is not true that I grudged the expense, but I *did* use a lamb instead of the ox. I suppose it was only natural that the people should have thought me miserly.'

'There is no harm in this. It is the way of a benevolent man. You saw the ox but not the lamb. The attitude of a gentleman towards animals is this: once having seen them alive, he cannot bear to see them die, and once having heard their cry, he cannot bear to eat their flesh. That is why the gentleman keeps his distance from the kitchen.'

The King was pleased and said, 'The *Odes* say,

> The heart is another man's,
> But it is I who have surmised it.[12]

This describes you perfectly. For though the deed was mine, when I looked into myself I failed to understand my own heart. You described it for me and your words struck a chord in me. What made you think that my heart accorded with the way of a true King?'

'Should someone say to you, "I am strong enough to lift a hundred *chün*[13] but not a feather; I have eyes that can see the tip of a new down but not a cartload of firewood," would you accept the truth of such a statement?'

'No.'

'Why should it be different in your own case? Your bounty is sufficient to reach the animals, yet the benefits of your government fail to reach the people. That a feather is not lifted is because one

曰：“不爲者與不能者之形何以異？”

曰：“挾太山以超北海，語人曰，‘我不能。’是誠不能也。爲長者折枝，語人曰，‘我不能。’是不爲也，非不能也。故王之不王，非挾太山以超北海之類也；王之不王，是折枝之類也。

“老吾老，以及人之老；幼吾幼，以及人之幼。天下可運於掌。詩云，‘刑于寡妻，至于兄弟，以御于家邦。’言舉斯心加諸彼而已。故推恩足以保四海，不推恩無以保妻子。古之人所以大過人者，無他焉，善推其所爲而已矣。今恩足以及禽獸，而功不至於百姓者，獨何與？

“權，然後知輕重；度，然後知長短。物皆然，心爲甚。王請度之！

“抑王興甲兵，危士臣，構怨於諸侯，然後快於心與？”

fails to make the effort; that a cartload of firewood is not seen is because one fails to use one's eyes. Similarly, that the people have not been tended is because you fail to practise kindness. Hence your failure to become a true King is due to a refusal to act, not to an inability to act.'

'What is the difference in form between refusal to act and inability to act?'

'If you say to someone, "I am unable to do it," when the task is one of striding over the North Sea with Mount T'ai under your arm, then this is a genuine case of inability to act. But if you say, "I am unable to do it," when it is one of making an obeisance to your elders, then this is a case of refusal to act, not of inability. Hence your failure to become a true King is not the same in kind as "striding over the North Sea with Mount T'ai under your arm", but the same as "making an obeisance to your elders".

'Treat the aged of your own family in a manner befitting their venerable age and extend this treatment to the aged of other families; treat your own young in a manner befitting their tender age and extend this to the young of other families, and you can roll the Empire on your palm.

'The *Odes* say,

> He set an example for his consort
> And also for his brothers,
> And so ruled over the family and the state.[14]

In other words, all you have to do is take this very heart here and apply it to what is over there. Hence one who extends his bounty can tend those within the Four Seas; one who does not cannot tend even his own family. There is just one thing in which the ancients greatly surpassed others, and that is the way they extended what they did. Why is it then that your bounty is sufficient to reach animals yet the benefits of your government fail to reach the people?

'It is by weighing a thing that its weight can be known and by measuring it that its length can be ascertained. It is so with all things, but particularly so with the heart. Your Majesty should measure his own heart.

'Perhaps you find satisfaction only in starting a war, imperilling

王曰：「否；吾何快於是？將以求吾所大欲也。」

曰：「王之所大欲可得聞與？」

王笑而不言。

曰：「為肥甘不足於口與？輕煖不足於體與？抑為采色不足視於目與？聲音不足聽於耳與？便嬖不足使令於前與？王之諸臣皆足以供之，而王豈為是哉？」

曰：「否；吾不為是也。」

曰：「然則王之所大欲可知已，欲辟土地，朝秦楚，莅中國而撫四夷也。以若所為求若所欲，猶緣木而求魚也。」

王曰：「若是其甚與？」

曰：「殆有甚焉。緣木求魚，雖不得魚，無後災。以若所為求若所欲，盡心力而為之，後必有災。」

曰：「可得聞與？」

曰：「鄒人與楚人戰，則王以為孰勝？」

曰：「楚人勝。」

曰：「然則小固不可以敵大，寡固不可以敵眾，弱固不可以敵強。海內之地方千里者九，齊集有其一。以一服八，何以異於鄒敵楚哉？蓋亦反其本矣。

「今王發政施仁，使天下仕者皆欲立於王之朝，耕者皆欲耕於王之野，商賈皆欲藏於王之市，行旅皆欲出於王之塗，天下之欲[1]疾其君者，皆欲赴愬於王。其若是，孰能禦之？」

[1] ‘欲疾’ 不辭。 ‘欲’ 字蓋衍文。

your subjects and incurring the enmity of other feudal lords?'

'No. Why should I find satisfaction in such acts? I only wish to realize my supreme ambition.'

'May I be told what this is?'

The King smiled, offering no reply.

'Is it because your food is not good enough to gratify your palate, and your clothes not good enough to gratify your body? Or perhaps the sights and sounds are not good enough to gratify your eyes and ears and your close servants not good enough to serve you? Any of your various officials surely could make good these deficiencies. It cannot be because of these things.'

'No. It is not because of these things.'

'In that case one can guess what your supreme ambition is. You wish to extend your territory, to enjoy the homage of Ch'in and Ch'u, to rule over the Central Kingdoms and to bring peace to the barbarian tribes on the four borders. Seeking the fulfilment of such an ambition by such means as you employ is like looking for fish by climbing a tree.'

'Is it as bad as that?' asked the King.

'It is likely to be worse. If you look for fish by climbing a tree, though you will not find it, there is no danger of this bringing disasters in its train. But if you seek the fulfilment of an ambition like yours by such means as you employ, after putting all your heart and might into the pursuit, you are certain to reap disaster in the end.'

'Can I hear about this?'

'If the men of Tsou and the men of Ch'u were to go to war, who do you think would win?'

'The men of Ch'u.'

'That means that the small is no match for the big, the few no match for the many, and the weak no match for the strong. Within the Seas there are nine areas of ten thousand *li* square, and the territory of Ch'i makes up one of these. For one to try to overcome the other eight is no different from Tsou going to war with Ch'u. Why not go back to fundamentals?

'Now if you should practise benevolence in the government of your state, then all those in the Empire who seek office would wish to find a place at your court, all tillers of land to till the land

王曰："吾惛，不能進於是矣。願夫子輔吾志，明以敎我。我雖不敏，請嘗試之。"

曰："無恆產而有恆心者，惟士爲能。若民，則無恆產，因無恆心。苟無恆心，放辟邪侈，無不爲已。及陷於罪，然後從而刑之，是罔民也。焉有仁人在位罔民而可爲也？是故明君制民之產，必使仰足以事父母，俯足以畜妻子，樂歲終身飽，凶年免於死亡；然後驅而之善，故民之從之也輕。

"今也制民之產，仰不足以事父母，俯不足以畜妻子；樂歲終身苦，凶年不免於死亡。此惟救死而恐不贍，奚暇治禮義哉？

"王欲行之，則盍反其本矣：五畝之宅，樹之以桑，五十者可以衣帛矣。雞豚狗彘之畜，無失其時，七十者可以食肉矣。百畝之田，勿奪其時，八口之家可以無飢矣。謹庠序之敎，申之以孝悌之義，頒白者不負戴於道路矣。老者衣帛食肉，黎民不飢不寒，然而不王者，未之有也。"

in outlying parts of your realm, all merchants to enjoy the refuge of your market-place, all travellers to go by way of your roads, and all those who hate their rulers to lay their complaints before you. This being so, who can stop you from becoming a true King?'

'I am dull-witted,' said the King, 'and cannot see my way beyond this point. I hope you will help me towards my goal and instruct me plainly. Though I am slow, I shall make an attempt to follow your advice.'

'Only a Gentleman can have a constant heart in spite of a lack of constant means of support. The people, on the other hand, will not have constant hearts if they are without constant means. Lacking constant hearts, they will go astray and fall into excesses, stopping at nothing. To punish them after they have fallen foul of the law is to set a trap for the people. How can a benevolent man in authority allow himself to set a trap for the people? Hence when determining what means of support the people should have, a clear-sighted ruler ensures that these are sufficient, on the one hand, for the care of parents, and, on the other, for the support of wife and children, so that the people always have sufficient food in good years and escape starvation in bad; only then does he drive them towards goodness; in this way the people find it easy to follow him.

'Nowadays, the means laid down for the people are sufficient neither for the care of parents nor for the support of wife and children. In good years life is always hard, while in bad years there is no way of escaping death. Thus simply to survive takes more energy than the people have. What time can they spare for learning about rites and duty?

'If you wish to put this into practice, why not go back to fundamentals? If the mulberry is planted in every homestead of five *mu* of land, then those who are fifty can wear silk; if chickens, pigs and dogs do not miss their breeding season, then those who are seventy can eat meat; if each lot of a hundred *mu* is not deprived of labour during the busy seasons, then families with several mouths to feed will not go hungry. Exercise due care over the education provided by village schools, and discipline the people by teaching them duties proper to sons and younger brothers, and

those whose heads have turned hoary will not be carrying loads on the roads. When the aged wear silk and eat meat and the masses are neither cold nor hungry, it is impossible for their prince not to be a true King.'

[12] Ode 198.
[13] Just under seven kilogrammes.
[14] Ode 240.

梁惠王章句下

1.　莊暴見孟子，曰：“暴見於王，王語暴以好樂，暴未有以對也。”
曰：“好樂何如？”

　　孟子曰：“王之好樂甚，則齊國其庶幾乎！”

　　他日，見於王曰：“王嘗語莊子以好樂，有諸？”

　　王變乎色，曰：“寡人非能好先王之樂也，直好世俗之樂耳。”

　　曰：“王之好樂甚，則齊其庶幾乎！今之樂猶古之樂也。”

　　曰：“可得聞與？”

　　曰：“獨樂樂，與人樂樂，孰樂？”

　　曰：“不若與人。”

　　曰：“與少樂樂，與眾樂樂，孰樂？”

　　曰：“不若與眾。”

　　“臣請為王言樂，今王鼓樂於此，百姓聞王鐘鼓之聲、管籥之
音，舉疾首蹙頞而相告曰：‘吾王之好鼓樂，夫何使我至於此極也？
父子不相見，兄弟妻子離散。’今王田獵於此，百姓聞王車馬之音，
見羽旄之美，舉疾首蹙頞而相告曰：‘吾王之好田獵，夫何使我至於
此極也？父子不相見，兄弟妻子離散。’此無他，不與民同樂也。

　　“今王鼓樂於此，百姓聞王鐘鼓之聲、管籥之音，舉欣欣然有喜
色而相告曰：‘吾王庶幾無疾病與，何以能鼓樂也？’今王田獵於此，
百姓聞王車馬之音，見羽旄之美，舉欣欣然有喜色而相告曰：‘吾王
庶幾無疾病與，何以能田獵也？’此無他，與民同樂也。今王與百姓
同樂，則王矣。”

BOOK I · PART B

1. Chuang Pao went to see Mencius. 'The King received me,' he said, 'and told me that he was fond of music. I was at a loss what to say.'

Then he added, 'What do you think of a fondness for music?'

'If the King has a great fondness for music,' answered Mencius, 'then there is perhaps hope for the state of Ch'i.'

Another day, when Mencius was received by the King, he said, 'Is it true that Your Majesty told Chuang Tzu that you were fond of music?'

The King blushed and said, 'It is not the music of the Former Kings that I am capable of appreciating. I am merely fond of popular music.'

'If you have a great fondness for music, then there is perhaps hope for the state of Ch'i. Whether it is the music of today or the music of antiquity makes no difference.'

'Can I hear more about this?'

'Which is greater, enjoyment[1] by yourself or enjoyment in the company of others?'

'In the company of others.'

'Which is greater, enjoyment in the company of a few or enjoyment in the company of many?'

'In the company of many.'

'Let me tell you about enjoyment. Now suppose you were having a musical performance here, and when the people heard the sound of your bells and drums and the notes of your pipes and flutes they all with aching heads and knitted brows said to one another. "Why does the King's fondness for music bring us to such straits that fathers and sons do not see each other, and brothers, wives and children are parted and scattered?" Again, suppose you were hunting here, and when the people heard the sound of your chariots and horses and saw the magnificence of your banners they all with aching heads and knitted brows said to one another, "Why does the King's fondness for hunting bring us to such straits that fathers and sons do not see each other, and brothers, wives and children are parted and scattered?" The reason would simply

2.　齊宣王問曰：“文王之囿方七十里，有諸？”

　　孟子對曰：“於傳有之。”

　　曰：“若是其大乎？”

　　曰：“民猶以爲小也。”

　　曰：“寡人之囿方四十里，民猶以爲大，何也？”

　　曰：“文王之囿方七十里，芻蕘者往焉，雉兔者往焉。與民同之。民以爲小，不亦宜乎？臣始至於境，問國之大禁，然後敢入。臣聞郊關之內有囿方四十里，殺其麋鹿者如殺人之罪。則是方四十里爲阱於國中。民以爲大，不亦宜乎？”

3.　齊宣王問曰：“交鄰國有道乎？”

　　孟子對曰：“有。惟仁者爲能以大事小，是故湯事葛，文王事昆

be that you failed to share your enjoyment with the people.

'On the other hand, suppose you were having a musical performance here, and when the people heard the sound of your bells and drums and the notes of your pipes and flutes they all looked pleased and said to one another, "Our King must be in good health, otherwise how could he have music performed?" Again, suppose you were hunting here, and when the people heard the sound of your chariots and horses and saw the magnificence of your banners they all looked pleased and said to one another, "Our King must be in good health, otherwise how could he go hunting?" The reason would again simply be that you shared your enjoyment with the people.

'Now if you shared your enjoyment with the people, you would be a true King.'

[1] Throughout this passage Mencius is exploiting the fact that the same graph is used both for 'music' and 'enjoyment'. It is to be expected that in some cases there is room for a difference of opinion as to whether the one or the other is meant.

2. King Hsüan of Ch'i asked, 'Is it true that the park of King Wen was seventy *li* square?'

'It is so recorded,' answered Mencius.

'Was it really as large as that?'

'Even so, the people found it small.'

'My park is only forty *li* square, and yet the people find it too big. Why is this?'

'True, King Wen's park was seventy *li* square, but it was open to woodcutters as well as catchers of pheasants and hares. As he shared it with the people, is it any wonder that they found it small?

'When I first arrived at the borders of your state, I inquired about the major prohibitions before I dared enter. I was told that within the outskirts of the capital there was a park forty *li* square in which the killing of a deer was as serious an offence as the killing of a man. This turns the park into a trap forty *li* square in the midst of the state. Is it any wonder that the people find it too big?'

3. King Hsüan of Ch'i asked, 'Is there a way of promoting good relations with neighbouring states?'

夷。惟智者爲能以小事大，故太王事獯鬻，勾踐事吳。以大事小者，樂天者也；以小事大者，畏天者也。樂天者保天下，畏天者保其國。詩云：‘畏天之威，于時保之。’”

王曰：“大哉言矣！寡人有疾，寡人好勇。”

對曰：“王請無好小勇。夫撫劍疾視曰，‘彼惡敢當我哉！’此匹夫之勇，敵一人者也，王請大之！

“詩云：‘王赫斯怒，爰整其旅，以遏徂莒，以篤周祜，以對于天下。’此文王之勇也。文王一怒而安天下之民。

“書曰：‘天降下民，作之君，作之師，惟曰其助上帝寵之。四方有罪無罪惟我在，天下曷敢有越厥志？’一人衡行於天下，武王恥之。此武王之勇也。而武王亦一怒而安天下之民。今王亦一怒而安天下之民，民惟恐王之不好勇也。”

'There is,' answered Mencius. 'Only a benevolent man can submit to a state smaller than his own. This accounts for the submission of T'ang to Ke and King Wen to the K'un tribes. Only a wise man can submit to a state bigger than his own. This accounts for the submission of T'ai Wang to the Hsün Yü and Kou Chien to Wu. He who submits to a state smaller than his own delights in Heaven; he who submits to a state bigger than his own is in awe of Heaven. He who delights in Heaven will continue to enjoy the possession of the Empire while he who is in awe of Heaven will continue to enjoy the possession of his own state. The *Odes* say,

> Being in awe of the majesty of Heaven
> We shall continue to enjoy our territory.[2]

'Great are your words,' said the King. 'but I have a weakness. I am fond of valour.'[3]

'I beg you not to be fond of small valour. To look fierce, putting your hand on your sword and say, "How dare he oppose me!" is to show the valour of a common fellow which is of use only against a single adversary. You should make it something great.

'The *Odes* say,

> The King blazed in rage
> And marshalled his troops
> To stop the enemy advancing on Chü
> And add to the good fortune of Chou
> In response to the wishes of the Empire.[4]

This was the valour of King Wen. In one outburst of rage King Wen brought peace to the people of the Empire.

'The *Book of History* says,

> Heaven sent the people down on earth,
> Made them a lord
> And made him their teacher
> That he might assist God in loving them.
> "In the four quarters, neither the innocent nor the guilty escape my eyes,
> Who in the Empire dare be above himself?"[5]

If there was one bully in the Empire, King Wu felt this to be a personal affront. This was the valour of King Wu. Thus he, too,

4.　齊宣王見孟子於雪宮。王曰：“賢者亦有此樂乎？”

孟子對曰：“有人不得，則非其上矣。不得而非其上者，非也；
爲民上而不與民同樂者，亦非也。樂民之樂者，民亦樂其樂；憂民之
憂者，民亦憂其憂。樂以天下，憂以天下，然而不王者，未之有也。

“昔者齊景公問於晏子曰：‘吾欲觀於轉附朝儛，遵海而南，放
於琅邪，吾何脩而可以比於先王觀也？’

“晏子對曰：‘善哉問也！天子適諸侯曰巡狩。巡狩者，巡所守
也。諸侯朝於天子曰述職。述職者，述所職也。無非事者。春省耕而
補不足，秋省斂而助不給。夏諺曰：‘吾王不遊，吾何以休？吾王不
豫，吾何以助？一遊一豫，爲諸侯度。’今也不然：師行而糧食，飢
者弗食，勞者弗息。睊睊胥讒，民乃作慝。方命虐民，飲食若流。流
連荒亡，爲諸侯憂。從流下而忘反謂之流，從流上而忘反謂之連，從
獸無厭謂之荒，樂酒無厭謂之亡。先王無流連之樂，荒亡之行。惟君
所行也。’

“景公說，大戒於國，出舍於郊。於是始興發補不足。召大師
曰：‘爲我作君臣相說之樂！’蓋徵招角招是也。其詩曰，‘畜君何
尤？’畜君者，好君也。”

brought peace to the people of the Empire in one outburst of rage.
Now if you, too, will bring peace to the people of the Empire in
one outburst of rage, then the people's only fear will be that you
are not fond of valour.'

² Ode 272.

³ The passage following is similar to two passages in I. B. 5 beginning 'I have a weak-
ness. I am fond of money' and 'I have a weakness. I am fond of women.' In *Hsin Hsü* 3/1
these passages form, in fact, a continuous whole.

⁴ Ode 241.

⁵ This is from the *T'ai shih*, one of the lost chapters of the *Book of History*, but has
been incorporated into the spurious chapter bearing the same title. See *Shu ching*, 11. 6a.

4. King Hsüan of Ch'i saw Mencius in the Snow Palace. 'Does even
a good and wise man,' asked the King, 'have such enjoyment as
this?'

'Should there be a man,'⁶ answered Mencius, 'who is not given
a share in such enjoyment, he would speak ill of those in authority.
To speak ill of those in authority because one is not given a share
in such enjoyment is, of course, wrong. But for one in authority
over the people not to share his enjoyment with the people is
equally wrong. The people will delight in the joy of him who
delights in their joy, and will worry over the troubles of him who
worries over their troubles. He who delights and worries on account
of the Empire is certain to become a true King.

'Once, Duke Ching of Ch'i asked Yen Tzu, "I wish to travel to
Chuan Fu and Ch'ao Wu, then to follow the Sea south to Lang
Yeh. What must I do to be able to emulate the travels of the
Former Kings?"

' "This is indeed a splendid question!" answered Yen Tzu. "When
the Emperor goes to the feudal lords, this is known as 'a tour of
inspection'. It is so called because its purpose is to inspect the
territories for which the feudal lords are responsible. When the
feudal lords go to pay homage to the Emperor, this is known as
'a report on duties'. It is so called because its purpose is to report
on duties they are charged with. Neither is undertaken without
good reason. In spring the purpose is to inspect ploughing so that
those who have not enough for sowing may be given help; in
autumn the purpose is to inspect harvesting so that those who are
in need may be given aid. As a saying of the Hsia Dynasty puts it:

5.　齊宣王問曰："人皆謂我毀明堂，毀諸？已乎？"

> If our King does not travel,
> How can we have rest?
> If our King does not go on tour,
> How can we have help?
> Every time he travels
> He sets an example for the feudal lords.

' "This is not so today:

> The army on the march live on dry provisions.
> The hungry do not get food;
> The weary do not get rest.
> They look askance and they complain.
> Thus the people begin to go astray.
> The lords misuse the people, going against the Decree.
> Food and drink flow like water.
> Drifting, lingering, rioting and intemperance,
> These excesses amongst the feudal lords are a cause for concern.

By 'drifting' is meant going downstream with no thought of returning; by 'lingering', going upstream with no thought of returning; by 'rioting', being insatiable in the hunt; by 'intemperance', being insatiable in drink. The Former Kings never undulged in any of these excesses. It is for you, my lord, to decide on your course of action."

'Duke Ching was pleased. He made elaborate preparations in the capital and then went to stay in the outskirts.[7] And then he opened up the granaries and gave to those who were needy. He summoned the Grand Musician and told him, "Make me music which expresses the harmony between ruler and subject." The result was the *Chih shao* and *Chüeh shao*. Here is the text,

> What is there reprehensible in pleasing the lord?

"To please the Lord" is "to be fond of him".'

[6]There is doubt as to how this sentence should be construed, as the text is most likely corrupt.

[7]i.e., he made preparations for giving help to the needy and marked the solemnity of the occasion by leaving the comforts of his palace.

5. King Hsüan of Ch'i asked, 'Everyone advises me to pull down

　　孟子對曰：“夫明堂者，王者之堂也。王欲行王政，則勿毀之矣。”

　　王曰：“王政可得聞與？”

　　對曰：“昔者文王之治岐也，耕者九一，仕者世祿，關市譏而不征，澤梁無禁，罪人不孥。老而無妻曰鰥，老而無夫曰寡，老而無子曰獨，幼而無父曰孤。此四者，天下之窮民而無告者。文王發政施仁，必先斯四者。詩云，‘哿矣富人，哀此煢獨。’”

　　王曰：“善哉言乎！”

　　曰：“王如善之，則何為不行？”

　　王曰：“寡人有疾，寡人好貨。”

　　對曰：“昔者公劉好貨，詩云，‘乃積乃倉，乃裹餱糧，于橐于囊。思戢用光。弓矢斯張，干戈戚揚，爰方啓行。’故居者有積倉，行者有裹囊也，然後可以爰方啓行。王如好貨，與百姓同之，於王何有？”

　　王曰：“寡人有疾，寡人好色。”

　　對曰：“昔者太王好色，愛厥妃。詩云：‘古公亶父，來朝走馬，率西水滸，至于岐下，爰及姜女，聿來胥宇。’當是時也，內無怨女，外無曠夫。王如好色，與百姓同之，於王何有？”

the Hall of Light. Should I or should I not do so?'

'The Hall of Light,' answered Mencius, 'is the hall of a true King. If Your Majesty wished to practise Kingly government, then he should not pull it down.'

'May I hear about Kingly government?'

'Formerly, when King Wen ruled over Ch'i,[8] tillers of land were taxed one part in nine;[9] descendants of officials received hereditary emoluments; there was inspection but no levy at border stations and market places;[10] fish-traps were open for all to use; punishment did not extend to the wife and children of an offender. Old men without wives, old women without husbands, old people without children, young children without fathers—these four types of people are the most destitute and have no one to turn to for help. Whenever King Wen put benevolent measures into effect, he always gave them first consideration. The *Odes* say,

> Happy are the rich;
> But have pity on the helpless.[11]

'Well spoken,' commented the King.

'If you consider my words well spoken, then why do you not put them into practice?'

'I have a weakness. I am fond of money.'

'In antiquity Kung Liu was fond of money too. The *Odes* say,

> He stocked and stored;
> He placed provisions
> In bags and sacks.
> He brought harmony and so glory to his state.
> On full display were bows and arrows,
> Spears, halberds and axes.
> Only then did the march begin.[12]

It was only when those who stayed at home had full granaries and those who went forth to war had full sacks that the march could begin. You may be fond of money, but so long as you share this fondness with the people, how can it interfere with your becoming a true King?'

'I have a weakness,' said the King. 'I am fond of women.'

'In antiquity, T'ai Wang was fond of women, and loved his

6.　孟子謂齊宣王曰："王之臣有託其妻子於其友而之楚遊者，比其反也，則凍餒其妻子，則如之何？"

　　王曰："棄之。"

　　曰："士師不能治士，則如之何？"

　　王曰："已之。"

　　曰："四境之內不治，則如之何？"

　　王顧左右而言他。

7.　孟子見齊宣王，曰："所謂故國者，非謂有喬木之謂也，有世臣之謂也。王無親臣矣，昔者所進，今日不知其亡也。"

　　王曰："吾何以識其不才而舍之？"

concubines. The *Odes* say,

> Ku Kung Tan Fu[13]
> Early in the morning galloped on his horse
> Along the banks of the river in the West
> Till he came to the foot of Mount Ch'i.
> He brought with him the Lady Chiang,
> Looking for a suitable abode.[14]

At that time, there were neither girls pining for a husband nor men without a wife. You may be fond of women, but so long as you share this fondness with the people, how can it interfere with your becoming a true King?'

[8]This is different from the state of Ch'i which figures so largely in this part of the book, though the romanization of the two names happens to be identical.

[9]i.e., the method of *chu* was used, by which eight families helped to cultivate the public land. Cf. III. A. 3.

[10]The text probably should read, 'there was inspection but no duty at border stations,' as is the case in II. A. 5. (p. 65).

[11]Ode 192.

[12]Ode 250.

[13]i.e., T'ai Wang.

[14]Ode 237.

6. Mencius said to King Hsüan of Ch'i, 'Suppose a subject of Your Majesty's, having entrusted his wife and children to the care of a friend, were to go on a trip to Ch'u, only to find, upon his return, that his friend had allowed his wife and children to suffer cold and hunger, then what should he do about it?'

'Break with his friend.'

'If the Marshal of the Guards was unable to keep his guards in order, then what should be done about it?'

'Remove him from office.'

'If the whole realm within the four borders was ill-governed, then what should be done about it?'

The King turned to his attendants and changed the subject.

7. Mencius went to see King Hsüan of Ch'i. 'A "state of established traditions",' said he, 'is so called not because it has tall trees but because it has ministers whose families have served it for generations. You no longer have trusted ministers. Those you promoted yester-

　　曰：“國君進賢，如不得已，將使卑踰尊，疏踰戚，可不愼與？左右皆曰賢，未可也；諸大夫皆曰賢，未可也；國人皆曰賢，然後察之；見賢焉，然後用之。左右皆曰不可，勿聽；諸大夫皆曰不可，勿聽；國人皆曰不可，然後察之；見不可焉，然後去之。左右皆曰可殺，勿聽；諸大夫皆曰可殺，勿聽；國人皆曰可殺，然後察之；見可殺焉，然後殺之。故曰，國人殺之也。如此，然後可以爲民父母。”

8.　　齊宣王問曰：“湯放桀，武王伐紂，有諸？”
　　　孟子對曰：“於傳有之。”
　　　曰：“臣弑其君，可乎？”
　　　曰：“賊仁者謂之‘賊’，賊義者謂之‘殘’。殘賊之人謂之‘一夫’。聞誅一夫紂矣，未聞弑君也。”

day have all disappeared today without your even being aware of it.'

'How could I have perceived,' said the King, 'that they lacked ability and so avoided making the appointments in the first instance?'

'When there is no choice, the ruler of a state, in advancing good and wise men, may have to promote those of low position over the heads of those of exalted rank and distant relatives over near ones. Hence such a decision should not be taken lightly. When your close attendants all say of a man that he is good and wise, that is not enough; when the Counsellors all say the same, that is not enough; when men in the capital all say so, then have the case investigated. If the man turns out to be good and wise, then and only then should he be given office. When your close attendants all say of a man that he is unsuitable, do not listen to them; when the Counsellors all say the same, do not listen to them; when men in the capital all say so, then have the case investigated. If the man turns out to be unsuitable, then and only then should he be removed from office. When your close attendants all say of a man that he deserves death, do not listen to them; when the Counsellors all say the same, do not listen to them; when men in the capital all say so, then have the case investigated. If the man turns out to deserve death, then and only then should he be put to death. In this way, it will be said, "He was put to death by men in the capital." Only by acting in this manner can one be father and mother to the people.'

8. King Hsüan of Ch'i asked, 'Is it true that T'ang banished Chieh and King Wu marched against Tchou?'[15]

'It is so recorded,' answered Mencius.

'Is regicide permissible?'

'He who mutilates benevolence is a mutilator; he who cripples rightness is a crippler; and a man who is both a mutilator and a crippler is an "outcast". I have indeed heard of the punishment of the "outcast Tchou", but I have not heard of any regicide.'

[15] It so happens that the name of the last emperor of the Shang Dynasty and the name of the dynasty which succeeded it come out in identical romanization. To avoid unnecessary confusion I have decided arbitrarily to use 'Tchou' for the tyrant, reserving 'Chou' for the dynasty.

9. 孟子謂齊宣王曰：“爲巨室，則必使工師求大木。工師得大木，則王喜，以爲能勝其任也。匠人斲而小之，則王怒，以爲不勝其任矣。夫人幼而學之，壯而欲行之，王曰，‘姑舍女所學而從我’，則何如？今有璞玉於此，雖萬鎰，必使玉人彫琢之。至於治國家，則曰，‘姑舍女所學而從我’，則何以異於敎玉人彫琢玉哉？”

10. 齊人伐燕，勝之。宣王問曰：“或謂寡人勿取，或謂寡人取之。以萬乘之國伐萬乘之國，五旬而舉之，人力不至於此。不取，必有天殃。取之，何如？”

  孟子對曰：“取之而燕民悅，則取之。古之人有行之者，武王是也。取之而燕民不悅，則勿取。古之人有行之者，文王是也。以萬乘之國伐萬乘之國，簞食壺漿以迎王師，豈有他哉？避水火也。如水益深，如火益熱，亦運而已矣。”

11. 齊人伐燕，取之。諸侯將謀救燕。宣王曰：“諸侯多謀伐寡人者，何以待之？”

9. Mencius said to King Hsüan of Ch'i. 'To build a big house,' said he, 'one has to ask the master carpenter to search for huge pieces of timber. If the master carpenter succeeds in finding such timber, the King will be pleased and consider him equal to his task. If the carpenter whittles down this timber, the King will be angry and consider him a bungler. A man, who, since his childhood, has been acquiring knowledge, naturally wishes to put this knowledge to use when he grows up. Now what would happen if the King were to say to him, "Just put aside what you have learned and do as I tell you"? Suppose we have here a piece of uncut jade. Even if its value is equivalent to ten thousand *yi*[16] of gold, you will still have to entrust its cutting to a jade-cutter. But when it comes to the government of your state, you say, "Just put aside what you have learned and do as I tell you." In what way is this different from teaching the jade-cutter his job?'

[16] A *yi* is just under 300 grammes.

10. The men of Ch'i attacked and defeated Yen. King Hsüan said, 'Some advise me against annexing Yen while others urge me to do so. The occupation of a state of ten thousand chariots by another of equal strength in a matter of fifty days is a feat which could not have been brought about by human agency alone. If I do not annex Yen, I am afraid Heaven will send down disasters. What would you think if I decided on annexation?'

'If in annexing Yen,' answered Mencius, 'you please its people, then annex it. There are examples of men in antiquity following such a course of action. King Wu was one. If in annexing Yen you antagonize its people, then do not annex it. There are also examples of men in antiquity following such a course. King Wen was one. When it is a state of ten thousand chariots attacking another of equal strength and your army is met by the people bringing baskets of rice and bottles of drink, what other reason can there be than that the people are fleeing from water and fire? Should the water become deeper and the fire hotter, they would have no alternative but to turn elsewhere for succour.'

11. The men of Ch'i attacked and annexed Yen. The feudal lords deliberated how they might go to the aid of Yen. King Hsüan said,

孟子對曰：“臣聞七十里爲政於天下者，湯是也。未聞以千里畏人者也。書曰：‘湯一征，自葛始。’天下信之，東面而征，西夷怨；南面而征，北狄怨，曰：‘奚爲後我？’民望之，若大旱之望雲霓也。歸市者不止，耕者不變，誅其君而弔其民，若時雨降。民大悅。書曰：‘徯我后，后來其蘇。’今燕虐其民，王往而征之，民以爲將拯己於水火之中也，簞食壺漿以迎王師。若殺其父兄，係累其子弟，毀其宗廟，遷其重器，如之何其可也？天下固畏齊之彊也，今又倍地而不行仁政，是動天下之兵也。王速出令，反其旄倪，止其重器，謀於燕衆，置君而後去之，則猶可及止也。”

'Most of the feudal lords are thinking of going to war with me. In what way can I stop this from happening?'

'I have heard,' answered Mencius, 'of one who gained ascendancy over the Empire from the modest beginning of seventy *li* square. Such a one was T'ang. I have never heard of anyone ruling over a thousand *li* being afraid of others.

'The *Book of History* says,

In his punitive expeditions T'ang began with Ke.[17]

With this he gained the trust of the Empire, and when he marched on the east, the western barbarians complained, and when he marched on the south, the northern barbarians complained. They all said, "Why does he not come to us first?"[18] The people longed for his coming as they longed for a rainbow in time of severe drought. Those who were going to market did not stop; those who were ploughing went on ploughing. He punished the rulers and comforted the people, like a fall of timely rain, and the people greatly rejoiced.[19]

'The *Book of History* says,

We await our Lord. When he comes we will be revived.[20]

'Now when you went to punish Yen which practised tyranny over its people, the people thought you were going to rescue them from water and fire, and they came to meet your army, bringing baskets of rice and bottles of drink. How can it be right for you to kill the old and bind the young, destroy the ancestral temples and appropriate the valuable vessels? Even before this, the whole Empire was afraid of the power of Ch'i. Now you double your territory without practising benevolent government. This is to provoke the armies of the whole Empire. If you hasten to order the release of the captives, old and young, leave the valuable vessels where they were, and take your army out after setting up a ruler in consultation with the men of Yen, it is still not too late to halt the armies of the Empire.'

[17]It is possible that this quotation is from the *T'ang cheng* ('Punitive Expeditions of T'ang'), one of the lost chapters of the *Book of History*.

[18]Cf. VII. B. 4.

[19]This passage, starting from 'With this he gained', seems also to be a quotation, though probably not from the *Book of History*.

12.　鄒與魯鬨。穆公問曰：“吾有司死者三十三人，而民莫之死也。
誅之，則不可勝誅；不誅，則疾視其長上之死而不救，如之何則可[1]？”

　　孟子對曰：“凶年饑歲，君之民老弱轉乎溝壑，壯者散而之四方
者，幾千人矣；而君之倉廩實，府庫充，有司莫以告，是上慢而殘下
也。曾子曰：‘戒之戒之！出乎爾者，反乎爾者也。’ 夫民今而後得
反之也。君無尤焉！君行仁政，斯民親其上，死其長矣。”

　　[1] ‘可’ 下原有 ‘也’ 字，但此句全書三見（I.A.15, I.B.14, I.B.15）均無 ‘也’ 字。
今據刪。

13.　滕文公問曰：“滕，小國也，間於齊、楚。事齊乎？事楚乎？”
　　孟子對曰：“是謀非吾所能及也。無已，則有一焉：鑿斯池也，
築斯城也，與民守之，效死而民弗去，則是可為也。”

14.　滕文公問曰：“齊人將築薛，吾甚恐，如之何則可？”
　　孟子對曰：“昔者大王居邠，狄人侵之，去之岐山之下居焉。非
擇而取之，不得已也。苟為善，後世子孫必有王者矣。君子創業垂
統，為可繼也。若夫成功，則天也。君如彼何哉？強為善而已矣。”

[20]Probably also from the *T'ang cheng*. For this whole passage, starting from the previous quotation from the *Book of History*, cf. III. B. 5.

12. There was a border clash between Tsou and Lu. Duke Mu of Tsou asked, 'Thirty-three of my officials died, yet none of my people would sacrifice their lives for them. If I punish them, there are too many to be punished. If I do not punish them, then there they were, looking on with hostility at the death of their superiors without going to their aid. What do you think is the best thing for me to do?'

'In years of bad harvest and famine,' answered Mencius, 'close on a thousand of your people suffered, the old and the young being abandoned in the gutter, the able-bodied scattering in all directions, yet your granaries were full and there was failure on the part of your officials to inform you of what was happening. This shows how callous those in authority were and how cruelly they treated the people. Tseng Tzu said, "Take heed! Take heed! What you mete out will be paid back to you." It is only now that the people have had an opportunity of paying back what they received. You should not bear them any grudge. Practise benevolent government and the people will be sure to love their superiors and die for them.'

13. Duke Wen of T'eng asked, 'T'eng is a small state, wedged between Ch'i and Ch'u. Should I be subservient to Ch'i or should I be subservient to Ch'u?'

'This is a question that is beyond me,' answered Mencius. 'If you insist, there is only one course of action I can suggest. Dig deeper moats and build higher walls and defend them shoulder to shoulder with the people. If they would rather die than desert you, then all is not lost.'

14. Duke Wen of T'eng asked, 'The men of Ch'i are going to fortify Hsüeh. I am greatly perturbed. What is the best thing for me to do?'

'In antiquity,' answered Mencius, 'T'ai Wang was in Pin. The Ti tribes invaded Pin and he left and went to settle at the foot of Mount Ch'i. He did this, not out of choice but because he had no alternative. If a man does good deeds, then amongst his descend-

15. 滕文公問曰：“滕，小國也；竭力以事大國，則不得免焉，如之何則可？”

　　孟子對曰：“昔者大王居邠，狄人侵之。事之以皮幣，不得免焉；事之以犬馬，不得免焉；事之以珠玉，不得免焉。乃屬其耆老而告之曰：‘狄人之所欲者，吾土地也。吾聞之也：君子不以其所以養人者害人。二三子何患乎無君？我將去之。’去邠，踰梁山，邑于岐山之下居焉。邠人曰：‘仁人也，不可失也。’從之者如歸市。

　　“或曰：‘世守也，非身之所能為也。効死勿去。’

　　“君請擇於斯二者。”

16. 魯平公將出，嬖人臧倉者請曰：“他日君出，則必命有司所之。今乘輿已駕矣，有司未知所之，敢請。”

　　公曰：“將見孟子。”

　　曰：“何哉，君所為輕身以先於匹夫者！以為賢乎？禮義由賢者出；而孟子之後喪踰前喪。君無見焉！”

　　公曰：“諾。”

　　樂正子入見，曰：“君奚為不見孟軻也？”

　　曰：“或告寡人曰：‘孟子之後喪踰前喪’，是以不往見也。”

　　曰：“何哉，君所謂踰者？前以士，後以大夫；前以三鼎，而後以五鼎與？”

　　曰：“否；謂棺椁衣衾之美也。”

　　曰：“非所謂踰也，貧富不同也。”

ants in future generations there will rise one who will become a true King. All a gentleman can do in starting an enterprise is to leave behind a tradition which can be carried on. Heaven alone can grant success. What can you do about Ch'i? You can only try your best to do good.'

15. Duke Wen of T'eng said, 'T'eng is a small state. If it tries with all its might to please the large states, it will only bleed itself white in the end. What is the best thing for me to do?'

'In antiquity,' answered Mencius, 'when T'ai Wang was in Pin, the Ti tribes invaded the place. He tried to buy them off with skins and silks; he tried to buy them off with horses and hounds; he tried to buy them off with pearls and jade; but all to no avail. Then he assembled the elders and announced to them, "What the Ti tribes want is our land. I have heard that a man in authority never turns what is meant for the sustenance of men into a source of harm to them. It will not be difficult for you, my friends, to find another lord. I am leaving." And he left Pin, crossed the Liang Mountains, built a city at the foot of Mount Ch'i and settled there. The men of Pin said, "This is a benevolent man. We must not lose him." They flocked after him as if to market.

'Others expressed the view, "This is the land of our forbears. It is not up to us to abandon it. Let us defend it to the death."

'You will have to choose between these two courses.'

16. Duke P'ing of Lu was about to go out. A favourite by the name of Tsang Ts'ang asked, 'My lord, on previous occasions when you went out you always gave instructions to the officials as to where you were going. Now the carriage is ready and the officials have not been told of your destination. May I be told about it?'

'I am going to see Mencius,' said the Duke.

'How extraordinary the reason for which you are lowering your-self in taking the initiative towards a meeting with a common fellow! If it is because you think him a good and wise man, a good and wise man is the source of the rites and what is right, yet with Mencius the second funeral [that is, of his mother] surpassed the first [that is, of his father]. My lord, I beg of you not to go to see him.'

'As you wish.'

　　樂正子見孟子，曰："克告於君，君爲來見也。嬖人有臧倉者沮君，君是以不果來也。"

　　曰："行，或使之；止，或尼之。行止，非人所能也。吾之不遇魯侯，天也。臧氏之子焉能使予不遇哉？"

Yüeh-cheng Tzu went in and asked, 'My lord, why did you not go to see Meng K'e?'

'Someone told me that with Mencius the second funeral surpassed the first. It was for that reason that I did not go.'

'How extraordinary that you should use the word "surpassed"! Is it because the second funeral was in a style appropriate to a mourner with the status of a Counsellor while the first was in a style appropriate to one with the status of only a Gentleman that you used the word "surpassed"? Or is it because in the second funeral five tripods of offerings were used while in the first three only were used?'

'No, I had in mind the superior quality of the coffins[21] and the clothes.'

'That is not a matter of "surpassing". It is simply a matter of being in more comfortable circumstances.'

Yüeh-cheng Tzu saw Mencius. 'I mentioned you to the prince,' said he, 'and he was to have come to see you. Amongst his favourites is one Tsang Ts'ang who dissuaded him. That is why he failed to come.'

'When a man goes forward, there is something which urges him on; when he halts, there is something which holds him back. It is not in his power either to go forward or to halt. It is due to Heaven that I failed to meet the Marquis of Lu. How can this fellow Tsang be responsible for my failure?'

[21]Cf. II. B. 7.

公孫丑章句上

1.　　公孫丑問曰："夫子當路於齊,管仲、晏子之功,可復許乎?"
　　孟子曰："子誠齊人也,知管仲、晏子而已矣。或問乎曾西曰:
'吾子與子路孰賢?'曾西蹵然曰:'吾先子之所畏也。'曰:'然
則吾子與管仲孰賢?'曾西艴然不悅,曰:"爾何曾比予於管仲?管
仲得君如彼其專也,行乎國政如彼其久也,功烈如彼其卑也;爾何曾
比予於是?'"曰:"管仲,曾西之所不為也,而子為我願之乎?"
　　曰:"管仲以其君霸,晏子以其君顯。管仲、晏子猶不足為與?"
　　曰:"以齊王,由反手也。"
　　曰:"若是,則弟子之惑滋甚。且以文王之德,百年而後崩,猶
未洽於天下;武王、周公繼之,然後大行。今言王若易然,則文王不
足法與?"

曰:文王何可當也?由湯至於武丁,賢聖之君六七作,天下歸殷
久矣,久則難變也。武丁朝諸侯,有天下,猶運之掌也。紂之去武丁
未久也,其故家遺俗,流風善政,猶有存者;又有微子、微仲、王子
比干、箕子、膠鬲——皆賢人也——相與輔相之,故久而後失之也。
尺地,莫非其有也;一民,莫非其臣也;然而文王猶方百里起,是以

BOOK II · PART A

1. Kung-sun Ch'ou asked, 'If you, Master, were to hold the reins of government in Ch'i, could a repetition of the success of Kuan Chung and Yen Tzu be predicted?'

'You are very much a native of Ch'i,' said Mencius, 'You know only of Kuan Chung and Yen Tzu.

'Someone once asked Tseng Hsi,[1] "My good sir, how do you compare with Tzu-lu?"

' "Even my late father held him in awe," answered Tseng Hsi, with an air of embarrassment.

' "In that case, how do you compare with Kuan Chung?"

'This time Tseng Hsi looked offended. "Why do you compare me with such a man as Kuan Chung?" he asked. "Kuan Chung enjoyed the confidence of his prince so exclusively and managed the affairs of state for so long, and yet his achievements were so insignificant. Why do you compare me with such a man?" '

Mencius then added, 'If it was beneath even Tseng Hsi to become a Kuan Chung, are you saying that I would be willing?'

'Kuan Chung made his prince leader of the feudal lords, and Yen Tzu made his illustrious. Are they not good enough for you to emulate?'

'To make the King of Ch'i a true King is as easy as turning over one's hand.'

'If that is the case, then I am more perplexed than ever. Virtuous as King Wen was, he did not succeed in extending his influence over the whole Empire when he died at the age of a hundred. It was only after his work was carried on by King Wu and the Duke of Chou that that influence prevailed. Now you talk as if becoming a true King were an easy matter. In that case, do you find King Wen an unworthy example?'

'How can I stand comparison with King Wen? From T'ang to Wu Ting, there were six or seven wise or sage kings, and the Empire was for long content to be ruled by the Yin. What has gone on for long is difficult to change. Wu Ting commanded the homage of the feudal lords and maintained the possession of the Empire as easily as rolling it on his palm.

難也。齊人有言曰：'雖有智慧，不如乘勢；雖有鎡基，不如待時。'今時則易然也：夏后、殷、周之盛，地未有過千里者也，而齊有其地矣；雞鳴狗吠相聞，而達乎四境，而齊有其民矣。地不改辟矣，民不改聚矣，行仁政而王，莫之能禦也。且王者之不作，未有疏於此時者也；民之憔悴於虐政，未有甚於此時者也。飢者易爲食，渴者易爲飲。孔子曰：'德之流行，速於置郵而傳命。'當今之時，萬乘之國行仁政，民之悅之，猶解倒懸也。故事半古之人，功必倍之，惟此時爲然。"

'Tchou was not far removed in time from Wu Ting. There still persisted traditions of ancient families and fine government measures handed down from earlier times. Furthermore, there were the Viscount of Wei, Wei Chung, Prince Pi Kan, the Viscount of Chi and Chiao Ke, all fine men, who assisted Tchou. That is why it took him such a long time to lose the Empire. There was not one foot of land which was not his territory, nor a single man who was not his subject. On the other hand, King Wen was just rising from a territory of only one hundred *li* square. That is why it was so difficult.

'The people of Ch'i have a saying,

> You may be clever,
> But it is better to make use of circumstances;
> You may have a hoe
> But it is better to wait for the right season.

The present is, however, an easy time.

'Even at the height of their power, the Hsia, Yin and Chou never exceeded a thousand *li* square in territory, yet Ch'i has the requisite territory. The sound of cocks crowing and dogs barking can be heard all the way to the four borders. Thus Ch'i has the requisite population. For Ch'i no further extension of its territory or increase of its population is necessary. The King of Ch'i can become a true King just by practising benevolent government, and no one will be able to stop him.

'Moreover, the appearance of a true King has never been longer overdue than today; and the people have never suffered more under tyrannical government than today. It is easy to provide food for the hungry and drink for the thirsty. Confucius said,

> The influence of virtue spreads
> Faster than setting up posting stations for orders to be transmitted.

'At the present time, if a state of ten thousand chariots were to practise benevolent government, the people would rejoice as if they had been released from hanging by the heels. Now is the time when one can, with half the effort, achieve twice as much as the ancients.'

---

[1] This Tseng Hsi was the younger son of Tseng Tzu, disciple of Confucius, not to be

2.　公孫丑問曰：“夫子加齊之卿相，得行道焉，雖由此霸王，不異矣。如此，則動心否乎？”

孟子曰：“否；我四十不動心。”

曰：“若是，則夫子過孟賁遠矣。”

曰：“是不難，告子先我不動心。”

曰：“不動心有道乎？”

曰：“有。北宮黝之養勇也：不膚橈，不目逃，思以一豪挫於人，若撻之於市朝；不受於褐寬博，亦不受於萬乘之君；視刺萬乘之君，若刺褐夫；無嚴諸侯，惡聲至，必反之。孟施舍之所養勇也，曰：‘視不勝猶勝也；量敵而後進，慮勝而後會，是畏三軍者也。舍豈能爲必勝哉？能無懼而已矣。’孟施舍似曾子，北宮黝似子夏。夫二子之勇，未知其孰賢，然而孟施舍守約也。昔者曾子謂子襄曰：‘子好勇乎？吾嘗聞大勇於夫子矣：自反而不縮，雖褐寬博，吾必[1]惴焉；自反而縮，雖千萬人，吾往矣。’孟施舍之守氣，又不如曾子之守約也。”

[1]‘必’原作‘不’，‘不’蓋‘必’之聲誤。今以意改。

confused with the Tseng Hsi mentioned in IV. A. 19, VII. B. 36 and VII. B. 37 who was Tseng Tzu's father. The Chinese names behind the apparent identity in romanization are quite different.

2. Kung-sun Ch'ou said, 'If you, Master, were given the responsibility of the Chief Minister in Ch'i and were able to put the Way into practice, it would be no surprise if through this you were able to make the King of Ch'i a leader of the feudal lords or even a true King. If this happened, would it cause any stirring in your heart?'

'No,' said Mencius. 'My heart has not been stirred since the age of forty.'

'In that case you far surpass Meng Pin.'

'That is not difficult. Kao Tzu succeeded in this at an even earlier age than I.'

'Is there a way to develop a heart that cannot be stirred?'

'Yes, there is. The way Po-kung Yu cultivated his courage was by never showing submission on his face or letting anyone out-stare him. For him, to yield the tiniest bit was as humiliating as to be cuffed in the market place. He would no more accept an insult from a prince with ten thousand chariots than from a common fellow coarsely clad. He would as soon run a sword through the prince as through the common fellow. He had no respect for persons, and always returned whatever harsh tones came his way.

'Meng Shih-she said this about the cultivation of his courage. "I look upon defeat as victory. One who advances only after sizing up the enemy, and joins battle only after weighing the chances of victory is simply showing cowardice in face of superior numbers. Of course I cannot be certain of victory. All I can do is to be without fear."

'Meng Shih-she resembled Tseng Tzu while Po-kung Yu resembled Tzu-hsia. It is hard to say which of the two was superior, but Meng Shih-she had a firm grasp of the essential.

'Tseng Tzu once said to Tzu-hsiang, "Do you admire courage? I once heard about supreme courage from the Master.[2] If, on looking within, one finds oneself to be in the wrong, then even though one's adversary be only a common fellow coarsely clad one is bound to tremble with fear. But if one finds oneself in the right, one goes forward even against men in the thousands." Meng Shih-she's firm hold on his *ch'i*[3] is inferior to Tseng Tzu's firm

曰：“敢問夫子之不動心與告子之不動心，可得聞與？”

“告子曰：‘不得於言，勿求於心；不得於心，勿求於氣。’不得於心，勿求於氣，可；不得於言，勿求於心，不可[2]。夫志，氣之帥也；氣，體之充也。夫志至焉，氣次焉；故曰：‘持其志，無暴其氣。’”

“既曰，‘志至焉，氣次焉，’又曰，‘持其志，無暴其氣’者，何也？”

曰：“志壹則動氣，氣壹則動志也。今夫蹶者趨者，是氣也，而反動其心。”

“敢問夫子惡乎長？”

曰：“我知言，我善養吾浩然之氣。”

“敢問何謂浩然之氣？”

曰：“難言也。其爲氣也，至大至剛，以直養而無害，則塞于天地之間。其爲氣也，配義與道；無是，餒也。是集義所生者，非義襲而取之也。行有不慊於心，則餒矣。我故曰，告子未嘗知義，以其外之也。必有事焉，而勿忘[3]。勿忘，勿助長也。無若宋人然：宋人有閔其苗之不長而揠之者，芒芒然歸，謂其人曰：‘今日病矣！予助苗長矣！’其子趨而往視之，苗則槁矣。天下之不助苗長者寡矣。以爲無益而舍之者，不耘苗者也；助之長者，揠苗者也——非徒無益，而又害之。”

---

[2] 《莊子·人間世》：无聽之以耳而聽之以心；无聽之以心而聽之以氣。(卷二頁八下至九上) 莊子之主張又與告子、孟子不同。

[3] ‘忘’字原作‘正心。’顧炎武《日知錄》引倪思說謂‘正心’應作‘忘’。(卷七頁十六下) 今據倪說改。

grasp of the essential.'

'I wonder if you could tell me something about the heart that cannot be stirred, in your case and in Kao Tzu's case?'

'According to Kao Tzu, "If you fail to understand words, do not worry about this in your heart; and if you fail to understand in your heart, do not seek satisfaction in your *ch'i*." It is right that one should not seek satisfaction in one's *ch'i* when one fails to understand in one's heart. But it is wrong to say that one should not worry about it in one's heart when one fails to understand words.

'The will is commander over the *ch'i* while the *ch'i* is that which fills the body. Where the will arrives there the *ch'i* halts. Hence it is said, "Take hold of your will and do not abuse your *ch'i*." '

'As you have already said that where the will arrives there the *ch'i* halts, what is the point of going on to say, "Take hold of your will and do not abuse your *ch'i*"?'

'The will, when blocked, moves the *ch'i*. On the other hand, the *ch'i*, when blocked, also moves the will. Now stumbling and hurrying affect the *ch'i*,[4] yet in fact palpitations of the heart are produced.'[5]

'May I ask what your strong points are?'

'I have an insight into words. I am good at cultivating my "flood-like *ch'i*".'

'May I ask what this "flood-like *ch'i*" is?'

'It is difficult to explain. This is a *ch'i* which is, in the highest degree, vast and unyielding. Nourish it with integrity and place no obstacle in its path and it will fill the space between Heaven and Earth. It is a *ch'i* which unites rightness and the Way. Deprive it of these and it will collapse. It is born of accumulated rightness and cannot be appropriated by anyone through a sporadic show of rightness. Whenever one acts in a way that falls below the standard set in one's heart, it will collapse. Hence I said Kao Tzu never understood rightness because he looked upon it as external.[6] You must work at it and never let it out of your mind. At the same time, while you must never let it out of your mind, you must not forcibly help it grow either. You must not be like the man from Sung.[7] There was a man from Sung who pulled at his seedlings because he was worried about their failure to grow. Having done so, he went on his way home, not realizing what he had done.

「何謂知言？」

曰：「詖辭知其所蔽，淫辭知其所陷，邪辭知其所離，遁辭知其所窮。──生於其心，害於其政；發於其政，害於其事。聖人復起，必從吾言矣。」

「宰我、子貢善爲說辭；冉牛、閔子、顏淵善言德行。孔子兼之，曰：『我於辭命，則不能也。』然則夫子旣聖矣乎？」

曰：「惡！是何言也？昔者子貢問於孔子曰：『夫子聖矣乎？』孔子曰：『聖則吾不能，我學不厭而教不倦也。』子貢曰：『學不厭，智也；教不倦，仁也。仁且智，夫子旣聖矣。』夫聖，孔子不居──是何言也？」

「昔者竊聞之：子夏、子游、子張皆有聖人之一體，冉牛、閔子、顏淵則具體而微，敢問所安。」

曰：「姑舍是。」

曰：「伯夷、伊尹何如？」

曰：「不同道。非其君不事，非其民不使；治則進，亂則退，伯夷也。何事非君，何使非民；治亦進，亂亦進，伊尹也。可以仕則仕，可以止則止，可以久則久，可以速則速，孔子也。皆古聖人也，吾未能有行焉；乃所願，則學孔子也。」

"I am worn out today," said he to his family. "I have been helping the seedlings to grow." His son rushed out to take a look and there the seedlings were, all shrivelled up. There are few in the world who can resist the urge to help their seedlings to grow. There are some who leave the seedlings unattended, thinking that nothing they can do will be of any use. They are the people who do not even bother to weed. There are others who help the seedlings grow. They are the people who pull at them. Not only do they fail to help them but they do the seedlings positive harm.'

'What do you mean by "an insight into words"?'

'From biased words I can see wherein the speaker is blind; from immoderate words, wherein he is ensnared; from heretical words, wherein he has strayed from the right path; from evasive words, wherein he is at his wits' end. What arises in the mind will interfere with policy, and what shows itself in policy will interfere with practice. Were a sage to rise again, he would surely agree with what I have said.'⁸

'Tsai Wo and Tzu-kung excelled in rhetoric; Jan Niu, Min Tzu and Yen Hui excelled in the exposition of virtuous conduct.⁹ Confucius excelled in both and yet he said, "I am not versed in rhetoric." In that case you, Master, must already be a sage.'

'What an extraordinary thing for you to say of me! Tzu-kung once asked Confucius, "Are you, Master, a sage?" Confucius replied, "I have not succeeded in becoming a sage. I simply never tire of learning nor weary of teaching." Tzu-kung said, "Not to tire of learning is wisdom; not to weary of teaching is benevolence. You must be a sage to be both wise and benevolent.¹⁰ A sage is something even Confucius did not claim to be. What an extraordinary thing for you to say of me!'

'I have heard that Tzu-hsia, Tzu-yu and Tzu-chang each had one aspect of the Sage while Jan Niu, Min Tzu and Yen Hui were replicas of the Sage in miniature. Which would you rather be?'

'Let us leave this question for the moment.'

'How about Po Yi and Yi Yin?'

'They followed paths different from that of Confucius. Po Yi was such that he would only serve the right prince and rule over the right people, took office when order prevailed and relinquished it when there was disorder. Yi Yin was such that he would serve

"伯夷、伊尹於孔子，若是班乎？"

曰："否；自有生民以來，未有孔子也。"

"然則有同與？"

曰："有。得百里之地而君之，皆能以朝諸侯，有天下；行一不義，殺一不辜，而得天下，皆不爲也。是則同。"

曰："敢問其所以異。"

曰："宰我、子貢、有若，智足以知聖人，汙不至阿其所好。宰我曰：'以予觀於夫子，賢於堯、舜遠矣。' 子貢曰：'見其禮而知其政，聞其樂而知其德，由百世之後，等百世之王，莫之能違也。自生民以來，未有夫子也。' 有若曰：'豈惟民哉？麒麟之於走獸，鳳凰之於飛鳥，泰山之於丘垤，河海之於行潦，類也。聖人之於民，亦類也。出於其類，拔乎其萃，自生民以來，未有盛於孔子也。'"

any prince and rule over any people, would take office whether
order prevailed or not. Confucius was such that he would take
office, or would remain in a state, would delay his departure or
hasten it, all according to circumstances.[11] All three were sages of
old. I have not been able to emulate any of them, but it is my
hope and wish to follow the example of Confucius.'

'Were Po Yi and Yi Yin as much an equal of Confucius as that?'

'No. Ever since man came into this world, there has never been
another Confucius.'

'Was there anything in common to all of them?'

'Yes. Were they to become ruler over a hundred *li* square, they
would have been capable of winning the homage of the feudal
lords and taking possession of the Empire; but had it been necessary
to perpetrate one wrongful deed or to kill one innocent man in
order to gain the Empire, none of them would have consented to
it. In this they were alike.'

'In what way were they different?'

'Tsai Wo, Tzu-kung and Yu Jo were intelligent enough to
appreciate the Sage.[12] They would not have stooped so low as to
show a bias in favour of the man they admired. Tsai Wo said, "In
my view, the Master surpassed greatly Yao and Shun." Tzu-kung
said, "Through the rites of a state he could see its government;
through its music, the moral quality of its ruler. Looking back over
a hundred generations he was able to appraise all the kings, and no
one has ever been able to show him to be wrong in a single instance.
Ever since man came into this world, there has never been another
like the Master." Yu Jo said, "It is true not only of men. The
unicorn is the same in kind as other animals, the phoenix as other
birds; Mount T'ai is the same as small mounds of earth; the Yellow
River and the Sea are no different from water that runs in the
gutter. The Sage, too, is the same in kind as other men.

> Though one of their kind
> He stands far above the crowd.

Ever since man came into this world, there has never been one
greater than Confucius." '

[2] i.e., Confucius.
[3] For a discussion of this term see Introduction p. xxii.

3.　孟子曰：“以力假仁者霸，霸必有大國；以德行仁者王，王不待
大——湯以七十里，文王以百里。以力服人者，非心服也，力不贍
也；以德服人者，中心悅而誠服也，如七十子之服孔子也。詩云：
‘自西自東，自南自北，無思不服。’此之謂也。”

4.　孟子曰：“仁則榮，不仁則辱；今惡辱而居不仁，是猶惡濕而居
下也。如惡之，莫如貴德而尊士，賢者在位，能者在職；國家閒暇，
及是時，明其政刑。雖大國，必畏之矣。詩云：‘迨天之未陰雨，徹
彼桑土，綢繆牖戶。今此下民，或敢侮予？’孔子曰：‘為此詩者，
其知道乎！能治其國家，誰敢侮之？’今國家閒暇，及是時，般樂怠
敖，是自求禍也。禍福無不自己求之者。詩云：‘永言配命，自求多
福。’太甲曰：‘天作孽，猶可違；自作孽，不可活。’此之謂也。”

[4] The *ch'i* here is the breath.

[5] This seems to be the end of this passage, with the rest of the section constituting a separate section.

[6] Cf. VI. A. 4.

[7] In the writings of the Warring States period the man from Sung was a byword for stupidity.

[8] The last part of this passage is found also in III. B. 9.

[9] Cf. The *Analects of Confucius*, XI.

[10] Cf. ibid., VII. 3. The version there seems less complete.

[11] Cf. V. B. 1.

[12] i.e., Confucius.

3. Mencius said, 'One who uses force while borrowing from benevolence will become leader of the feudal lords,[13] but to do so he must first be the ruler of a state of considerable size. One who puts benevolence into effect through the transforming influence of morality will become a true King, and his success will not depend on the size of his state. T'ang began with only seventy *li* square, and King Wen with a hundred. When people submit to force they do so not willingly but because they are not strong enough. When people submit to the transforming influence of morality they do so sincerely, with admiration in their hearts. An example of this is the submission of the seventy disciples to Confucius. The *Odes* say,

> From east, from west,
> From north, from south,
> There was none who did not submit.[14]

This describes well what I have said.'

[13] Cf. VII. A. 30.
[14] Ode 244.

4. Mencius said, 'Benevolence brings honour; cruelty, disgrace. Now people who dwell in cruelty while disliking disgrace are like those who are content to dwell in a low-lying place while disliking dampness. If one dislikes disgrace, one's best course of action is to honour virtue and to respect Gentlemen. If, when good and wise men are in high office and able men are employed, a ruler takes advantage of times of peace to explain the laws to the people, then even large states will certainly stand in awe of him. The *Odes* say,

> While it has not yet clouded over and rained,

5.　孟子曰：“尊賢使能，俊傑在位，則天下之士皆悅，而願立於其朝矣；市，廛而不征，法而不廛，則天下之商皆悅，而願藏於其市矣；關，譏而不征，則天下之旅皆悅，而願出於其路矣；耕者，助而不稅，則天下之農皆悅，而願耕於其野矣；廛，無夫里之布，則天下之民皆悅，而願為之氓矣。信能行此五者，則鄰國之民仰之若父母矣。率其子弟，攻其父母，自有生民以來未有能濟者也。如此，則無敵於天下。無敵於天下者，天吏也。然而不王者，未之有也。”

> I take the bark of the mulberry
> And bind fast the windows.
> Now none of the people
> Will dare treat me with insolence.[15]

Confucius' comment was: "The writer of this poem must have understood the Way. If a ruler is capable of putting his state in order, who would dare treat him with insolence?"

'Now a ruler who takes advantage of times of peace to indulge in pleasure and indolence is courting disaster. There is neither good nor bad fortune which man does not bring upon himself. The *Odes* say,

> Long may he be worthy of Heaven's Mandate
> And seek for himself much good fortune.[16]

The *T'ai Chia* says,

> When Heaven sends down calamities,
> There is hope of weathering them;
> When man brings them upon himself,
> There is no hope of escape.[17]

This describes well what I have said.'

[13] Cf. VII. A. 30.

[14] Ode 244.

[15] Ode 155. This ode is entitled *Ch'ih hsiao* ('Kite-owl') and is written in the first person, representing a bird persecuted by the kite-owl.

[16] Ode 235.

[17] The *T'ai Chia* is one of the lost chapters of the *Book of History*. This quotation has been incorporated into the spurious chapter of the same title in the present text. See *Shu ching*, 8. 21a.

5. Mencius said, 'If you honour the good and wise and employ the able so that outstanding men are in high position, then Gentlemen throughout the Empire will be only too pleased to serve at your court. In the market-place, if goods are exempted when premises are taxed, and premises exempted when the ground is taxed, then the traders throughout the Empire will be only too pleased to store their goods in your market-place. If there is inspection but no duty at the border stations, then the travellers throughout the Empire will be only too pleased to go by way of your roads. If

6.　孟子曰：“人皆有不忍人之心。先王有不忍人之心，斯有不忍人之政矣。以不忍人之心，行不忍人之政，治天下可運之掌上。所以謂人皆有不忍人之心者，今人乍見孺子將入於井，皆有怵惕惻隱之心——非所以內交於孺子之父母也，非所以要譽於鄉黨朋友也，非惡其聲而然也。由是觀之，無惻隱之心，非人也；無羞惡之心，非人也；無辭讓之心，非人也；無是非之心，非人也。惻隱之心，仁之端也；羞惡之心，義之端也；辭讓之心，禮之端也；是非之心，智之端也。人之有是四端也，猶其有四體也。有是四端而自謂不能者，自賊者也；謂其君不能者，賊其君者也。凡有四端於我者，知皆擴而充之矣，若火之始然，泉之始達。苟能充之，足以保四海；苟不充之，不足以事父母。”

tillers help in the public fields but pay no tax on the land, then farmers throughout the Empire will be only too pleased to till the land in your realm. If you abolish the levy in lieu of corvée and the levy in lieu of the planting of the mulberry, then all the people of the Empire will be only too pleased to come and settle in your state. If you can truly execute these five measures, the people of your neighbouring states will look up to you as to their father and mother; and since man came into this world no one succeeded in inciting children against their parents. In this way, you will have no match in the Empire. He who has no match in the Empire is a Heaven-appointed officer, and it has never happened that such a man failed to become a true King.'

6. Mencius said, 'No man is devoid of a heart sensitive to the suffering of others. Such a sensitive heart was possessed by the Former Kings and this manifested itself in compassionate government. With such a sensitive heart behind compassionate government, it was as easy to rule the Empire as rolling it on your palm.

'My reason for saying that no man is devoid of a heart sensitive to the suffering of others is this. Suppose a man were, all of a sudden, to see a young child on the verge of falling into a well. He would certainly be moved to compassion, not because he wanted to get in the good graces of the parents, nor because he wished to win the praise of his fellow villagers or friends, nor yet because he disliked the cry of the child. From this it can be seen that whoever is devoid of the heart of compassion is not human, whoever is devoid of the heart of shame is not human, whoever is devoid of the heart of courtesy and modesty is not human, and whoever is devoid of the heart of right and wrong is not human. The heart of compassion is the germ of benevolence; the heart of shame, of dutifulness; the heart of courtesy and modesty, of observance of the rites; the heart of right and wrong, of wisdom. Man has these four germs just as he has four limbs. For a man possessing these four germs to deny his own potentialities is for him to cripple himself; for him to deny the potentialities of his prince is for him to cripple his prince. If a man is able to develop all these four germs that he possesses, it will be like a fire starting up or a spring coming through. When these are fully developed, he can tend the

7.　孟子曰：“矢人豈不仁於函人哉？矢人惟恐不傷人，函人惟恐傷
人。巫匠亦然。故術不可不愼也。孔子曰：‘里仁爲美。擇不處仁，
焉得智？’夫仁，天之尊爵也，人之安宅也。莫之禦而不仁，是不智
也。不仁、不智，無禮、無義，人役也。人役而恥爲役，由弓人而恥
爲弓，矢人而恥爲矢也。如恥之，莫如爲仁。仁者如射：射者正己而
後發；發而不中，不怨勝己者，反求諸己而已矣。”

8.　孟子曰：“子路，人告之以有過則喜。禹聞善言則拜。大舜有大
焉，善與人同，捨己從人，樂取於人以爲善。自耕稼、陶、漁以至爲
帝，無非取於人者。取諸人以爲善，是與人爲善者也。故君子莫大乎
與人爲善。”

9.　孟子曰：“伯夷，非其君，不事；非其友，不友。不立於惡人之

whole realm within the Four Seas, but if he fails to develop them, he will not be able even to serve his parents.'

7. Mencius said, 'Is the maker of arrows really more unfeeling than the maker of armour? The maker of arrows is afraid lest he should fail to harm people, whereas the maker of armour is afraid lest they should be harmed. The case is similar with the sorcerer-doctor and the coffin-maker. For this reason one cannot be too careful in the choice of one's calling.

'Confucius said, "The best neighbourhood is where benevolence is to be found. Not to live in such a neighbourhood when one has the choice cannot by any means be considered wise."[18] Benevolence is the high honour bestowed by Heaven and the peaceful abode of man. Not to be benevolent when nothing stands in the way is to show a lack of wisdom. A man neither benevolent nor wise, devoid of courtesy and dutifulness, is a slave. A slave ashamed of serving is like a maker of bows ashamed of making bows, or a maker of arrows ashamed of making arrows. If one is ashamed, there is no better remedy than to practise benevolence. Benevolence is like archery: an archer makes sure his stance is correct before letting fly the arrow, and if he fails to hit the mark, he does not hold it against his victor. He simply seeks the cause within himself.'

[18] Cf. the *Analects of Confucius*, **IV**. I.

8. Mencius said, 'When anyone told him that he had made a mistake, Tzu-lu was delighted. When he heard a fine saying, Yü bowed low before the speaker. The Great Shun was even greater. He was ever ready to fall into line with others, giving up his own ways for theirs, and glad to take from others that by which he could do good. From the time he was a farmer, a potter and a fisherman to the time he became Emperor, there was nothing he did that he did not take from others. To take from others that by which one can do good is to help them do good. Hence there is nothing more important to a gentleman than helping others do good.'

9. Mencius said, 'Po Yi would serve only the right prince and

朝，不與惡人言；立於惡人之朝，與惡人言，如以朝衣朝冠坐於塗
炭。推惡惡之心，思與鄉人立，其冠不正，望望然去之，若將浼焉。
是故諸侯雖有善其辭命而至者，不受也。不受也者，是亦不屑就已。
柳下惠不羞汙君，不卑小官；進不隱賢，必以其道；遺佚而不怨，阨
窮而不憫。故曰，‘爾為爾，我為我，雖袒裼裸裎於我側，爾焉能浼
我哉？’故由由然與之偕而不自失焉，援而止之而止。援而止之而止
者，是亦不屑去已。”孟子曰：“伯夷隘，柳下惠不恭。隘與不恭，
君子不由也。”

befriend only the right man. He would not take his place at the court of an evil man, nor would he converse with him. For him to do so would be like sitting in mud and pitch wearing a court cap and gown. He pushed his dislike for evil to the extent that, if a fellow-villager in his company had his cap awry, he would walk away without even a backward look, as if afraid of being defiled. Hence even when a feudal lord made advances in the politest language, he would repel them. He repelled them simply because it was beneath him to go to the feudal lord.

'Liu Hsia Hui, on the other hand, was not ashamed of a prince with a tarnished reputation, neither did he disdain a modest post. When in office, he did not conceal his own talent, and always acted in accordance with the Way. When he was passed over he harboured no grudge, nor was he distressed even in straitened circumstances. That is why he said,[19] "You are you and I am I. Even if you were to be stark naked by my side, how could you defile me?" Consequently, he was in no hurry to take himself away, and looked perfectly at ease in the other man's company, and would stay when pressed. He stayed when pressed, simply because it was beneath him to insist on leaving.'

Mencius added, 'Po Yi was too straight-laced; Liu Hsia Hui was not dignified enough. A gentleman would follow neither extreme.'

[19] In place of 'that is why he said,' the parallel passage in V. B. 1 has the sentence 'when he was with a fellow-villager he simply could not tear himself away.' In the present passage, this sentence must have dropped out by mistake, as without it what follows becomes quite unintelligible.

公孫丑章句下

1. 孟子曰："天時不如地利，地利不如人和。三里之城，七里之郭，環而攻之而不勝。夫環而攻之，必有得天時者矣；然而不勝者，是天時不如地利也。城非不高也，池非不深也，兵革非不堅利也，米粟非不多也；委而去之，是地利不如人和也。故曰：域民不以封疆之界，固國不以山谿之險，威天下不以兵革之利。得道者多助，失道者寡助。寡助之至，親戚畔之；多助之至，天下順之。以天下之所順，攻親戚之所畔；故君子有不戰，戰必勝矣。"

2. 孟子將朝王，王使人來曰："寡人如就見者也，有寒疾，不可以風。朝，將視朝，不識可使寡人得見乎？"

對曰："不幸而有疾，不能造朝。"

明日，出弔於東郭氏。公孫丑曰："昔者辭以病，今日弔，或者不可乎？"

BOOK II · PART B

1. Mencius said, 'Heaven's favourable weather is less important than Earth's advantageous terrain, and Earth's advantageous terrain is less important than human unity.[1] Suppose you laid siege to a city with inner walls measuring, on each side, three *li* and outer walls measuring seven *li*, and you failed to take it. Now in the course of the siege, there must have been, at one time or another, favourable weather, and in spite of that you failed to take the city. This shows that favourable weather is less important than advantageous terrain. Sometimes a city has to be abandoned in spite of the height of its walls and depth of its moat, the quality of arms and abundance of food supplies. This shows that advantageous terrain is less important than human unity.

'Hence it is said, It is not by boundaries that the people are confined, it is not by difficult terrain that a state is rendered secure, and it is not by superiority of arms that the Empire is kept in awe. One who has the Way will have many to support him; one who has not the Way will have few to support him. In extreme cases, the latter will find even his own flesh and blood turning against him while the former will have the whole Empire at his behest. Hence either a gentleman does not go to war or else he is sure of victory, for he will have the whole Empire at his behest, while his opponent will have even his own flesh and blood turning against him.'

[1] Mencius is here claiming for Man an importance greater even than Heaven and Earth.

2. Mencius was about to go to court to see the King when a messenger came from the King with the message, 'I was to have come to see you, but I am suffering from a chill and cannot be exposed to the wind. In the morning I shall, however, be holding court. I wonder if I shall have the opportunity of seeing you then.' To this Mencius replied, 'Unfortunately, I too am ill and shall be unable to come to court.'

The next day, Mencius went on a visit of condolence to the Tung-kuo family. Kung-sun Ch'ou said, 'Yesterday you excused yourself on the ground of illness, yet today you go on a visit of

曰：“昔者疾，今日愈，如之何不弔？”

王使人問疾，醫來。

孟仲子對曰：“昔者有王命，有采薪之憂，不能造朝。今病小愈，趨造於朝，我不識能至否乎？”

使數人要於路，曰：“請必無歸，而造於朝！”

不得已而之景丑氏宿焉。

景子曰：“內則父子，外則君臣，人之大倫也。父子主恩，君臣主敬。丑見王之敬子也，未見所以敬王也。”

曰：“惡！是何言也！齊人無以仁義與王言者，豈以仁義爲不美也？其心曰，‘是何足與言仁義也’云爾，則不敬莫大乎是。我非堯舜之道，不敢以陳於王前，故齊人莫如我敬王也。”

景子曰：“否；非此之謂也。禮曰，‘父召，無諾；君命召，不俟駕。’固將朝也，聞王命而遂不果，宜與夫禮若不相似然。”

曰：“豈謂是與？曾子曰：‘晉楚之富，不可及也；彼以其富，我以吾仁；彼以其爵，我以吾義，吾何慊乎哉？’夫豈不義而曾子言之？是或一道也。天下有達尊三：爵一，齒一，德一。朝廷莫如爵，鄉黨莫如齒，輔世長民莫如德。惡得有其一以慢其二哉？故將大有爲之君，必有所不召之臣；欲有謀焉，則就之。其尊德樂道，不如是，不足與有爲也。故湯之於伊尹，學焉而後臣之，故不勞而王；桓公之於管仲，學焉而後臣之，故不勞而霸。今天下地醜德齊，莫能相尚，無他，好臣其所教，而不好臣其所受教。湯之於伊尹，桓公之於管仲，則不敢召。管仲且猶不可召，而況不爲管仲者乎？”

condolence. Would this not be improper?'

'I was ill yesterday, but I am recovered today. Why should I not go on a visit of condolence?'

The King sent someone to inquire after Mencius' illness; and a doctor came. Meng Chung-tzu in reply to the inquiry said, 'Yesterday when the King's summons came, Mencius was ill and was unable to go to court. Today he is somewhat better and has hastened to court. But I am not sure if, in his condition, he is able to get there.'

Then several men were sent to waylay Mencius with the message, 'Do not, under any circumstances, come home but go straight to court.'

Mencius was forced to go and spend the night with the Ching-ch'ou family.

'Within the family,' said Ching Tzu, 'the relationship between father and son is the most important, while outside, it is that between prince and subject. The former exemplifies love, the latter respect. I have seen the King show you respect, but I have yet to see you show the King respect.'

'What a thing to say! None of the men of Ch'i ever talks to the King about benevolence and rightness. Do you think it is because they do not think these beautiful? It is simply because, in their hearts, they say to themselves something to this effect, "How can we talk to *him* about benevolence and rightness?" There is nothing more lacking in respect than that. I have never dared put before the King anything short of the way of Yao and Shun. That is why no man from Ch'i respects the King as much as I.'

'No,' said Ching Tzu. 'That is not what I had in mind. According to the rites, "When summoned by one's father, one should not answer, I am coming.² When summoned by one's prince, one should not wait for the horses to be yoked to one's carriage." You were, in the first instance, about to go to court, but on being summoned by the King you changed your mind. This would seem to be contrary to the rites.'

'Is that what you meant? Tseng Tzu said, "The wealth of Chin and Ch'u cannot be rivalled. They may have their wealth, but I have my benevolence; they may have their exalted rank, but I have my integrity. In what way do I suffer in the comparison?" If this

3.　陳臻問曰：“前日於齊，王餽兼金一百，而不受；於宋，餽七十鎰而受；於薛，餽五十鎰而受。前日之不受是，則今日之受非也；今日之受是，則前日之不受非也。夫子必居一於此矣。”

　　孟子曰：“皆是也。當在宋也，予將有遠行，行者必以贐；辭曰：‘餽贐’予何爲不受？當在薛也，予有戒心；辭曰：‘聞戒，故爲兵餽之。’予何爲不受？若於齊，則未有處也。無處而餽之，是貨之也。焉有君子而可以貨取乎？”

is not right, Tseng Tzu would not have said it. It must be a possible way of looking at the matter. There are three things which are acknowledged by the world to be exalted: rank, age and virtue. At court, rank is supreme; in the village, age; but for assisting the world and ruling over the people it is virtue. How can a man, on the strength of the possession of one of these, treat the other two with arrogance? Hence a prince who is to achieve great things must have subjects he does not summon. If he wants to consult them, he goes to them. If he does not honour virtue and delight in the Way in such a manner, he is not worthy of being helped towards the achievement of great things. Take the case of Yi Yin. T'ang had him first as a tutor and only afterwards did he treat him as a minister. As a result, T'ang was able to become a true King without much effort. Again, take the case of Kuan Chung. Duke Huan treated him in exactly the same way and, as a result, was able to become a leader of the feudal lords without much effort. Today there are many states, all equal in size and virtue, none being able to dominate the others. This is simply because the rulers are given to employing those they can teach rather than those from whom they can learn. T'ang did not dare summon Yi Yin, nor did Duke Huan dare summon Kuan Chung. Even Kuan Chung could not be summoned, much less someone who would not be a Kuan Chung.'[3]

[2] but go immediately.
[3] Cf. II. A. 1.

3. Ch'en Chen asked, "The other day in Ch'i the King presented you with a hundred *yi* of gold of superior quality and you refused, but in Sung you were presented with seventy *yi* and you accepted; in Hsüeh you likewise accepted fifty *yi*. If your refusal in the first instance was right, then your acceptance on subsequent occasions must be wrong; on the other hand, if your acceptance was right, your refusal must be wrong. You cannot escape one or the other of these two alternatives.'

'Both refusal and acceptance were right,' said Mencius. 'When I was in Sung, I was about to go on a long journey, and for a traveller there is always a parting gift. The accompanying note said, "Presented as a parting gift." Why then should I have refused? In Hsüeh, I had to take precautions for my safety. The message

4.　孟子之平陸，謂其大夫曰：“子之持戟之士，一日而三失伍，則去之否乎？”

曰：“不待三。”

“然則子之失伍也亦多矣。凶年饑歲，子之民，老羸轉於溝壑，壯者散而之四方者，幾千人矣。”

曰：“此非距心之所得爲也。”

曰：“今有受人之牛羊而爲之牧之者，則必爲之求牧與芻矣。求牧與芻而不得，則反諸其人乎？抑亦立而視其死與？”

曰：“此則距心之罪也。”

他日，見於王曰：“王之爲都者，臣知五人焉。知其罪者，惟孔距心。爲王誦之。”

王曰：“此則寡人之罪也。”

5.　孟子謂蚔鼃曰：“子之辭靈丘而請士師，似也，爲其可以言也。今既數月矣，未可以言與？”

蚔鼃諫於王而不用，致爲臣而去。

齊人曰：“所以爲蚔鼃則善矣；所以自爲，則吾不知也。”

公都子以告。

曰：“吾聞之也：有官守者，不得其職則去；有言責者，不得其言則去。我無官守，我無言責也，則吾進退，豈不綽綽然有餘裕哉？”

accompanying the gift said, "I hear that you are taking precautions for your safety. This is a contribution towards the expenses of acquiring arms." Again, why should I have refused? But in the case of Ch'i I had no justification for accepting a gift. To accept a gift without justification is tantamount to being bought. Surely a gentleman should never allow himself to be bought.'

4. Mencius went to P'ing Lu. 'Would you or would you not,' said he to the governor, 'dismiss a lancer who has failed three times in one day to report for duty?'

'I would not wait for the third time.'

'But you yourself have failed to report for duty many times. In years of famine close on a thousand of your people suffered, the old and the young being abandoned in the gutter, the able-bodied scattered in all directions.'[4]

'It was not within my power to do anything about this.'

'Supposing a man were entrusted with the care of cattle and sheep. Surely he ought to seek pasturage and fodder for the animals. If he found that this could not be done, should he return his charge to the owner or should he stand by and watch the animals die?'

'In this I am at fault.'

On another day Mencius saw the King. 'Of the officials who are in charge of your provinces,' said he, 'I know five. The only one who realizes his own fault is K'ung Chü-hsin. I am, therefore, repeating our conversation for you.'

'In this I am really the one at fault,' said the King.

[4] Cf. I. B. 12, where this is given as the reason for the cold antipathy shown by the people towards those in authority.

5. Mencius said to Ch'ih Wa, 'When you gave up the governorship of Ling Ch'iu and requested to be made Marshal of the Guards your decision seemed right, as your new position offered opportunities for giving advice. That was several months ago. Have you not found an opportunity to speak yet?'

Ch'ih Wa offered advice to the King and tendered his resignation when this was not followed.

'Mencius gave splendid advice to Ch'ih Wa,' said the men of

6. 孟子爲卿於齊，出弔於滕，王使蓋大夫王驩爲輔行。王驩朝暮見，反齊滕之路，未嘗與之言行事也。

公孫丑曰："齊卿之位，不爲小矣；齊滕之路，不爲近矣，反之而未嘗與言行事，何也？"

曰："夫既或治之，予何言哉？"

7. 孟子自齊葬於魯，反於齊，止於嬴。

充虞請曰："前日不知虞之不肖，使虞敦匠事。嚴，虞不敢請。今願竊有請也：木若以美然。"

曰："古者棺椁無度，中古棺七寸，椁稱之。自天子達於庶人，非直爲觀美也，然後盡於人心。不得，不可以爲悅；無財，不可以爲悅。得之爲有財，古之人皆用之，吾何爲獨不然？且比化者無使土親膚，於人心獨無恔乎？吾聞之：君子不以天下儉其親。"

Ch'i, 'but we have yet to hear of him giving as good advice to himself.'

Kung-tu Tzu reported this to Mencius. 'I have heard,' said Mencius, 'that one who holds an office will resign it if he is unable to discharge his duties, and one whose responsibility is to give advice will resign if he is unable to give it. I hold no office, neither have I any responsibility for giving advice. Why should I not have plenty of scope when it comes to the question of staying or leaving?'

6. When Mencius was a Minister of Ch'i he went on a mission of condolence to T'eng. The King of Ch'i made Wang Huan, the governor of Ke, his deputy. Wang Huan went to see Mencius morning and evening, but throughout the journeys to and from T'eng, Mencius never discussed official business with him.

'Your position as Minister of Ch'i,' asked Kung-sun Ch'ou, 'is by no means insignificant, and the distance between Ch'i and T'eng is by no means short, yet throughout the journeys between the two states you never discussed official business with Wang Huan. Why was that?'

'He has managed the whole affair. What was there for me to say?'

7. Mencius returned from Ch'i to Lu for the burial [of his mother], and, on his way back to Ch'i, he put up at Ying.

'Some days ago,' ventured Ch'ung Yü, 'you did not think me unworthy and entrusted me with the task of overseeing the carpenters. As the work was urgent, I did not dare ask questions. May I ask a question now? The wood seemed to be excessively fine in quality.'[5]

'In high antiquity, there were no regulations governing the inner and outer coffins. In middle antiquity,[6] it was prescribed that the inner coffin was to be seven inches thick with the outer coffin to match. This applied to all conditions of men, from Emperor to Commoner. This is not simply for show. It is only in this way that one can express fully one's filial love. However, if such wood is not available, one cannot have the satisfaction of using it; neither can one if one is unable to afford the cost. When

8.　沈同以其私問曰：“燕可伐與？”

　　孟子曰：“可；子噲不得與人燕，子之不得受燕於子噲。有仕於此，而子悅之，不告於王而私與之吾子之祿爵；夫士也，亦無王命而私受之於子，則可乎？——何以異於是？”

　　齊人伐燕。

　　或問曰：“勸齊伐燕，有諸？”

　　曰：“未也；沈同問‘燕可伐與’，吾應之曰，‘可’，彼然而伐之也。彼如曰，‘孰可以伐之？’ 則將應之曰，‘為天吏，則可以伐之。’ 今有殺人者，或問之曰，‘人可殺與？’則將應之曰，‘可。’彼如曰，‘孰可以殺之？’ 則將應之曰：‘為士師，則可以殺之。’ 今以燕伐燕，何為勸之哉？”

both conditions are fulfilled, the ancients always used wood of fine quality. Why should I alone be an exception? Furthermore, does it not give one some solace to be able to prevent the earth from coming into contact with the dead who is about to decompose? I have heard it said that a gentleman would not for all the world skimp on expenditure where his parents are concerned.'

[5] This same criticism was used by Mencius' enemies to discredit him. See I. B. 16.

[6] According to K'ung Kuang-sen, 'middle antiquity' should be taken to refer to a time before the Duke of Chou, as the different classes came under different regulations according to the rites of the Chou. See his *Ching hsüeh chih yen* (*Huang Ch'ing ching chieh* 715.2a)

8. Shen T'ung asked on his own account, 'Is it all right to march on Yen?'

'Yes,' answered Mencius. 'Tzu-k'uai had no right to give Yen[7] to another; neither had Tzu-chih any right to accept it from Tzu-k'uai. Supposing there were a Gentleman here whom you liked and you were to take it upon yourself to give him your emolument and rank without informing the King, and he, for his part, were to accept these from you without royal sanction. Would this be permissible? The case of Yen is no different from this.'

The men of Ch'i marched on Yen.

'Is it true,' someone asked Mencius, 'that you encouraged Ch'i to march on Yen?'

'No. When Shen T'ung asked me, "Is it all right to march on Yen?" I answered, "Yes." And they marched on Yen. Had he asked, "Who has the right to march on Yen?" I would have answered, "A Heaven-appointed officer has the right to do so." Suppose a man killed another, and someone were to ask, "Is it all right to kill the killer?" I would answer, "Yes." But if he further asked, "Who has the right to kill him?" I would answer, "The Marshal of the Guards has the right to kill him." As it is, it is just one Yen marching on another Yen. Why should I have encouraged such a thing?'

[7] In 315 B.C. King K'uai of Yen abdicated in favour of his prime minister Tzu-chih. This sparked off an armed conflict in Yen, and it was at this point that King Hsüan of Ch'i intervened. Apart from this and the next section, I. B. 10 and I. B. 11 also refer to this affair.

9.　燕人畔。王曰：“吾甚慙於孟子。”

陳賈曰：“王無患焉。王自以爲與周公孰仁且智？”

王曰：“惡！是何言也！”

曰：“周公使管叔監殷，管叔以殷畔；知而使之，是不仁也；不知而使之，是不智也。仁智，周公未之盡也，而況於王乎？賈請見而解之。”

見孟子，問曰：“周公何人也？”

曰：“古聖人也。”

曰：“使管叔監殷，管叔以殷畔也，有諸？”

曰：“然。”

曰：“周公知其將畔而使之與？”

曰：“不知也。”

“然則聖人且有過與？”

曰：“周公，弟也；管叔，兄也。周公之過，不亦宜乎？且古之君子，過則改之；今之君子，過則順之。古之君子，其過也，如日月之食，民皆見之；及其更也，民皆仰之。今之君子，豈徒順之，又從爲之辭。”

10.　孟子致爲臣而歸。王就見孟子，曰：“前日願見而不可得，得侍同朝，甚喜；今又棄寡人而歸，不識可以繼此而得見乎？”

9. The men of Yen rose in rebellion. The King of Ch'i said, 'I am very much ashamed to face Mencius.'

'You should not let this affair worry you,' said Ch'en Chia. 'Which do you think a wiser and more benevolent man, the Duke of Chou or yourself?'

'What a thing to ask!'

'The Duke of Chou made Kuan Shu overlord of Yin and Kuan Shu used it as a base to stage a rebellion. If the Duke of Chou sent Kuan Shu knowing what was going to happen, then he was not benevolent; if he sent him for lack of foresight, then he was unwise. Even the Duke of Chou left something to be desired in the matter of benevolence and wisdom. How much more in the case of Your Majesty. May I be permitted to go and disabuse Mencius' mind?'

He went to see Mencius. 'What sort of a man,' he asked, 'was the Duke of Chou?'

'A sage of antiquity.'

'Is it true that he made Kuan Shu overlord of Yin and Kuan Shu used it to stage a rebellion?'

'Yes.'

'Did the Duke send him, knowing that he was going to stage a rebellion?'

'No. He did not.'

'In that case even a sage makes mistakes.'

'The Duke of Chou was the younger brother of Kuan Shu. Is it not natural for him to have made such a mistake? Furthermore, when he made a mistake, the gentleman of antiquity would make amends, while the gentleman of today persists in his mistakes. When the gentleman of antiquity made a mistake it was there to be seen by all the people, like the eclipse of the sun and the moon; and when he made amends the people looked up to him.[8] The gentleman of today not only persists in his mistakes but tries to gloss over them.'

[8] Cf. the *Analects of Confucius*, XIX. 21.

10. Mencius was going to go home, having resigned from office. The King went to see him. 'Previously,' said the King, 'I wished in vain to meet you. Then I had the opportunity of attending you in the

對曰：“不敢請耳，固所願也。”

他日，王謂時子曰：“我欲中國而授孟子室，養弟子以萬鍾，使諸大夫國人皆有所矜式。子盍爲我言之！”

時子因陳子而以告孟子，陳子以時子之言告孟子。

孟子曰：“然；夫時子惡知其不可也？如使予欲富，辭十萬而受萬，是爲欲富乎？季孫曰：‘異哉子叔疑！使己爲政，不用，則亦已矣，又使其子弟爲卿。人亦孰不欲富貴？而獨於富貴之中有私龍斷焉。’古之爲市也，以其所有易其所無者，有司者治之耳。有賤丈夫焉，必求龍斷而登之，以左右望，而罔市利。人皆以爲賤，故從而征之。征商自此賤丈夫始矣。”

11，孟子去齊，宿於晝。有欲爲王留行者，坐而言。不應，隱几而臥。

客不悅曰：“弟子齊宿而後敢言，夫子臥而不聽，請勿復敢見矣。”

曰：“坐！我明語子。昔者魯繆公無人乎子思之側，則不能安子思；泄柳、申詳無人乎繆公之側，則不能安其身。子爲長者慮，而不及子思；子絕長者乎？長者絕子乎？”

same court, much to my delight. Now you abandon me and go home. I wonder if I shall have further opportunities of seeing you?'

'That is just what I should wish,' answered Mencius, 'though I did not dare make the suggestion.'

On another day, the King said to Shih Tzu. 'I wish to give Mencius a house in the most central part of my capital and a pension of ten thousand measures of rice for the support of his disciples, so that the officials and the men of the capital will have an example to look up to. Why do you not sound him out for me?'

Shih Tzu informed Mencius of this through Ch'en Tzu. When Mencius heard Shih Tzu's message through Ch'en Tzu, he said, 'I see. But then Shih Tzu cannot be expected to realize that this cannot be done. Do you think that I am after wealth? If I were, would I give up a hundred thousand measures and accept ten thousand instead?

'Chi Sun once said, "How odd Tzu-shu Yi was! His advice was not followed while he was in office. This did not prevent him from getting the younger members of his family into high office. Who is there that does not want wealth and rank? But he was the only one that had his own 'vantage point' therein." In antiquity, the market was for the exchange of what one had for what one lacked. The authorities merely supervised it. There was, however, a despicable fellow who always looked for a vantage point and, going up on it, gazed into the distance to the left and to the right in order to secure for himself all the profit there was in the market. The people all thought him despicable, and, as a result, they taxed him. The taxing of traders began with this despicable fellow.'

11. Mencius left Ch'i and on his way put up at Chou. There was a man who wished to persuade Mencius to stay on behalf of the King. He sat upright and began to speak, but Mencius made no reply and lay down, leaning against the low table.

The visitor was displeased. 'Only after observing a day's fast,' said he, 'dare I speak. You, Master, simply lie down and make no effort to listen to me. I shall never dare present myself again.'

'Be seated. I shall speak to you plainly. In the time of Duke Mu

12. 孟子去齊。尹士語人曰："不識王之不可以爲湯武，則是不明
也；識其不可，然且至，則是干澤也。千里而見王，不遇故去，三宿
而後出晝，是何濡滯也？士則茲不悅。"

高子以告。

曰："夫尹士惡知予哉？千里而見王，是予所欲也；不遇故去，
豈予所欲哉？予不得已也。予三宿而出晝，於予心猶以爲速，王庶幾
改之！王如改諸[1]，則必反予。夫出晝，而王不予追也，予然後浩然
有歸志。予雖然，豈舍王哉！王由足用爲善；王如用予，則豈徒齊民
安，天下之民舉安。王庶幾改之！予日望之！予豈若是小丈夫然哉？
諫於其君而不受，則怒，悻悻然見於其面，去則窮日之力而後宿哉？"
尹士聞之，曰："士誠小人也。"

[1] 審文義，'改諸' 應作 '改之'，上句 '改之' 應作 '改諸'，'諸' '之'二字
誤易。《風俗通義‧窮通篇》（頁318）正作'王庶幾改諸，王如改之。'按下文'王
庶幾改之！予日望之！《論衡‧刺孟》（卷十頁十三上）引 '之'作 '諸'。

of Lu, if he did not have one of his own men close to Tzu-ssu he could not have kept Tzu-ssu happy. On the other hand, Hsieh Liu and Shen Hsiang remained secure only by having one of their own friends close to the Duke. You, my son, are trying to arrange things on my behalf, yet you fall short of following the example of Tzu-ssu. Are you refusing to have anything to do with me, or am I refusing to have anything to do with you?'

12. After Mencius left Ch'i, Yin Shih said to someone, 'If he did not realize that the King could not become a T'ang or a King Wu he was blind, but if he came realizing it, he was simply after advancement. He came a thousand *li* to see the King, and left because he met with no success. It took him three nights to go beyond Chou. Why was he so long about it? I for one find this most distasteful.'

Kau Tzu[9] told Mencius of this. 'How little,' said Mencius, 'does Yin Shih understand me. I came a thousand *li* to see the King because I wanted to. Having met with no success, I am leaving, not because I want to but because I have no alternative. True, it took me three nights to go beyond Chou. But even then I felt that I had not taken long enough. I had hoped against hope that the King would change his mind. I was sure he would recall me if this happened. It was only when I went beyond Chou and the King made no attempt to send after me that the desire to go home surged up in me. Even then it was not as if I had abandoned the King. The King is still capable of doing good. If the King had employed me, it would not simply be a matter of bringing peace to the people of Ch'i, but of bringing peace to the people of the whole Empire as well. If only the King would change his mind: that is what I hope for every day. I am not like those petty men who, when their advice is rejected by the prince, take offence and show resentment all over their faces, and, when they leave, travel all day before they would put up for the night.'

Yin Shih, on hearing this, said, 'I am indeed a petty man.'

---

[9]There are at least three people whose names come out in romanization as 'Kao Tzu'. To avoid confusion, I have decided arbitrarily to reserve 'Kao Tzu' for the philosopher who discusses the problem of human nature with Mencius in Book VI. For the others I use the spelling 'Kau'. The 'Kau Tzu' here is probably the same as the 'Kau Tzu' who

13. 孟子去齊，充虞路問曰：「夫子若有不豫色然。前日虞聞諸夫子曰：『君子不怨天，不尤人。』」

　　曰：「彼一時，此一時也。五百年必有王者興，其間必有名世者。由周而來，七百有餘歲矣。以其數，則過矣；以其時考之，則可矣。夫天未欲平治天下也；如欲平治天下，當今之世，舍我其誰也？吾何為不豫哉？」

14. 孟子去齊，居休。公孫丑問曰：「仕而不受祿，古之道乎？」

　　曰：「非也；於崇，吾得見王，退而有去志，不欲變，故不受也。繼而有師命，不可以請。久於齊，非我志也。」

appears in VII. B. 21 and VII. B. 22, while the 'Kau Tzu' who figures in VI. B. 3 seems to be an older man and so a different person.

13. When Mencius left Ch'i, on the way Ch'ung Yü asked, 'Master, you look somewhat unhappy. I heard from you the other day that a gentleman reproaches neither Heaven nor man.'

'This is one time; that was another time. Every five hundred years a true King should arise, and in the interval there should arise one from whom an age takes its name. From Chou to the present, it is over seven hundred years. The five hundred mark is passed; the time seems ripe. It must be that Heaven does not as yet wish to bring peace to the Empire. If it did, who is there in the present time other than myself? Why should I be unhappy?'

14. Mencius left Ch'i and stayed at Hsiu. Kung-sun Ch'ou asked, 'Is it ancient practice to take office without accepting pay?'

'No. In Ch'ung after I had my first audience with the King, I already had the intention of leaving. It was because I did not want to have to change my mind subsequently that I did not accept pay in the first place. It so happened that war broke out and I had no opportunity of requesting permission to leave. It never was my intention to remain long in Ch'i.'

滕文公章句上

1.　滕文公爲世子，將之楚，過宋而見孟子。孟子道性善，言必稱堯舜。

　　世子自楚反，復見孟子。孟子曰：“世子疑吾言乎？夫道一而已矣。成覸謂齊景公曰：‘彼，丈夫也；我，丈夫也；吾何畏彼哉？’顏淵曰：‘舜，何人也？予，何人也？有爲者亦若是。’ 公明儀曰：‘文王，我師也；周公豈欺我哉？’今滕，絕長補短，將五十里也，猶可以爲善[1]。書曰：‘若藥不瞑眩，厥疾不瘳。’”

> [1] ‘善’下原有‘國’字。IIB 13 ‘王由足用爲善’，句法與此相同，但‘善’下無‘國’字。今據刪。

2.　滕定公薨，世子謂然友曰：“昔者孟子嘗與我言於宋，於心終不忘。今也不幸至於大故，吾欲使子問於孟子，然後行事。”

　　然友之鄒問於孟子。

　　孟子曰：“不亦善乎！親喪，固所自盡也。曾子曰：‘生，事之以禮；死，葬之以禮，祭之以禮，可謂孝矣。’諸侯之禮，吾未之學也；雖然，吾嘗聞之矣。三年之喪，齊疏之服，飦粥之食，自天子達於庶人，三代共之。”

BOOK III · PART A

1. Duke Wen of T'eng, while still crown prince, was once going to Ch'u. While passing through Sung, he saw Mencius who talked to him about the goodness of human nature, always citing as his authorities Yao and Shun.

On the way back from Ch'u the crown prince again saw Mencius.

'Does Your Highness doubt my words?' asked Mencius. 'There is one Way and one only. Ch'eng Chien said to Duke Ching of Ch'i, "He is a man and I am a man. Why should I be in awe of him?" Similarly, Yen Hui said, "What sort of a man was Shun? And what sort of a man am I? Anyone who can make anything of himself will be like that." Kung-ming Yi said, "When he said that he modelled himself on King Wen, surely the Duke of Chou was not trying to take us in?"

'Now if you reduce T'eng to a regular shape, it would have a territory of almost fifty *li* square. It is big enough for you to do good.

'The *Book of History* says,

If the medicine does not make the head swim, the illness will not be cured.'[1]

[1] This saying is also to be found in the *Kuo yü* (17. 10b) where it is said to be from the *Book of Wu Ting*. It has been incorporated into the spurious *Yüeh Ming I* of the present *Shu ching* (10. 3a).

2. Duke Ting of T'eng died. The crown prince said to Jan Yu, 'I have never been able to forget what Mencius once said to me in Sung. Now that I have had the misfortune to lose my father, I want you to go and ask Mencius' advice before making funeral arrangements.'

Jan Yu went to Tsou to ask Mencius' advice.

'Splendid,' said Mencius. 'The funeral of a parent is an occasion for giving of one's utmost.[2] Tseng Tzu said, "When your parents are alive, comply with the rites in serving them; when they die, comply with the rites in burying them; comply with the rites in sacrificing to them; and you deserve to be called a good son."[3] I am afraid I am not conversant with the rites observed by the

　　然友反命，定爲三年之喪。父兄百官皆不欲，曰："吾宗國魯先君莫之行，吾先君亦莫之行也，至於子之身而反之，不可。且志曰：'喪祭從先祖。'"曰，"吾有所受之也。"

　　謂然友曰："吾他日未嘗學問，好馳馬試劍。今也父兄百官不我足也，恐其不能盡於大事，子爲我問孟子！"

　　然友復之鄒問孟子。

　　孟子曰："然；不可以他求者也。孔子曰：'君薨，聽於冢宰，歠粥，面深墨，即位而哭，百官有司莫敢不哀，先之也。　上有好者，下必有甚焉者矣。君子之德，風也；小人之德，草也。草尙之風，必偃。'是在世子。"

　　然友反命。

　　世子曰："然；是誠在我。"

　　五月居廬，未有命戒。百官族人可，謂曰知[1]。及至葬，四方來觀之，顏色之戚，哭泣之哀，弔者大悅。

---

[1] 朱子曰："'可謂曰知，'疑有闕誤。'《孟子集注》（卷五頁四上）

feudal lords. Still, I have heard something about funeral rites. Three years as the mourning period, mourning dress made of rough hemp with a hem, the eating of nothing but rice gruel— these were observed in the Three Dynasties by men of all conditions alike, from Emperor to Commoner.'

Jan Yu reported this to the crown prince, and it was decided to observe the three-year mourning period. The elders and all the officials were opposed to this and said, 'The ancestral rulers of the eldest branch of our house in Lu never observed this; neither did our own ancestral rulers. Now it comes to you, and you go against our accepted practice. This is perhaps ill-advised. Furthermore, the *Records* say, "In funeral and sacrifice, one follows the practice of one's ancestors." ' They added, 'We have authority for what we do.'

The crown prince said to Jan Yu, 'In the past I have never paid much attention to learning, caring only for riding and fencing. Now the elders and all my officials do not think too highly of me, and I am afraid they may not give of their best in this matter. Go and consult Mencius for me.'

Jan Yu went once again to Tsou to ask Mencius for advice.

'I see,' said Mencius. 'But in this matter the solution cannot be sought elsewhere. Confucius said, "When the ruler dies the heir entrusts his affairs to the steward[4] and sips rice gruel, showing a deep inky colour on his face. He then takes his place and weeps, and none of his numerous officials dare show a lack of grief. This is because he sets the example. When someone above shows a preference for anything, there is certain to be someone below who will outdo him. The virtue of the gentleman is like wind; the virtue of the small man is like grass. Let the wind blow over the grass, and it is sure to bend."[5] It rests with the crown prince.'

Jan Yu reported on his mission.

'That is so,' said the crown prince. 'It does, indeed, rest with me.'

For five months he stayed in his mourning hut, issuing no orders or prohibitions. The officials and his kinsmen approved of his actions and thought him well-versed in the rites. When it was time for the burial ceremony, people came from all quarters to watch. He showed such a grief-stricken countenance and wept so bitterly that the mourners were greatly delighted.

3.   滕文公問爲國。

孟子曰：“民事不可緩也。詩云：‘晝爾于茅，宵爾索綯；亟其乘屋，其始播百穀。’民之爲道也，有恆產者有恆心，無恆產者無恆心。苟無恆心，放辟邪侈，無不爲已。及陷乎罪，然後從而刑之，是罔民也。焉有仁人在位罔民而可爲也？是故賢君必恭儉禮下，取於民有制。陽虎曰：‘爲富不仁矣，爲仁不富矣。’

“夏后氏五十而貢，殷人七十而助，周人百畝而徹，其實皆什一也。徹者，徹也；助者，藉也。龍子曰：‘治地莫善於助，莫不善於貢。’貢者，校數歲之中以爲常。樂歲，粒米狼戾，多取之而不爲虐，則寡取之；凶年，糞其田而不足，則必取盈焉。爲民父母，使民盻盻然，將終歲勤動，不得以養其父母，又稱貸而益之，使老稚轉乎溝壑，惡在其爲民父母也？夫世祿，滕固行之矣。詩云：‘雨我公田，遂及我私。’惟助爲有公田。由此觀之，雖周亦助也。

[2] Cf. the *Analects of Confucius*, XIX. 17.
[3] Cf. ibid., II. 5, where the saying is attributed to Confucius.
[4] Cf. ibid., XIV. 4.
[5] Cf. ibid., XII. 19.

3. Duke Wen of T'eng asked about government.

'The business of the people,' said Mencius, 'must be attended to without delay. The *Odes* say,

> In the day time they go for grass;
> At night they make it into ropes.
> They hasten to repair the roof;
> Then they begin sowing the crops.[6]

This is the way of the common people. Those with constant means of support will have constant hearts, while those without constant means will not have constant hearts. Lacking constant hearts, they will go astray and get into excesses, stopping at nothing. To punish them after they have fallen foul of the law is to set a trap for the people. How can a benevolent man in authority allow himself to set a trap for the people?[7] Hence a good ruler is always respectful and thrifty, courteous and humble, and takes from the people no more than is prescribed. Yang Hu said, "If one's aim is wealth one cannot be benevolent; if one's aim is benevolence one cannot be wealthy."

'In the Hsia Dynasty, each family was given fifty *mu* of land, and the "*kung*" method of taxation was used; in the Yin, each family was given seventy *mu* and the "*chu*" method was used; in the Chou, each family was given a hundred *mu* and the "*ch'e*" method was used. In fact, all three amounted to a taxation of one in ten. "*Ch'e*" means "commonly practised"; "*chu*" means "to lend help". Lung Tzu said, "In administering land, there is no better method than *chu* and no worse than *kung*." With the *kung* method, the payment due is calculated on the average yield over a number of years. In good years when rice is so plentiful that it goes to waste, the people are no more heavily taxed, though this would mean no hardship; while in bad years, when there is not enough to spare for fertilizing the fields, the full quota is insisted upon. If he who is father and mother to the people makes it

　　"設爲庠序學校以敎之。庠者，養也；校者，敎也；序者，射也。夏曰校，殷曰序，周曰庠；學則三代共之，皆所以明人倫也。人倫明於上，小民親於下。有王者起，必來取法，是爲王者師也。

　　"詩云：'周雖舊邦，其命惟新。' 文王之謂也。子力行之，亦以新子之國！"

　　使畢戰問井地。

　　孟子曰："子之君將行仁政，選擇而使子，子必勉之！夫仁政，必自經界始。經界不正，井地不鈞，穀祿不平，是故暴君汙吏必慢其經界。經界旣正，分田制祿可坐而定也。

necessary for them to borrow because they do not get enough to minister to the needs of their parents in spite of having toiled incessantly all the year round, and causes the old and young to be abandoned in the gutter, wherein is he father and mother to the people?

'Hereditary emolument as a matter of fact is already practised in T'eng.

'The *Odes* say,

> The rain falls on our public land,
> And so also on our private land.[8]

There is "public land" only when *chu* is practised. From this we see that even the Chou practised *chu.*[9]

' *"Hsiang"*, *"hsü"*, *"hsüeh"* and *"hsiao"* were set up for the purpose of education. *"Hsiang"* means "rearing", *"hsiao"* means "teaching" and *"hsü"* means "archery".[10] In the Hsia Dynasty it was called *"hsiao"*, in the Yin *"hsü"* and in the Chou *"hsiang"*, while *"hsüeh"* was a name common to all the Three Dynasties. They all serve to make the people understand human relationships.[11] When it is clear that those in authority understand human relationships, the people will be affectionate. Should a true King arise, he is certain to take this as his model. Thus he who practises this will be tutor to a true King.

'The *Odes* say,

> Though Chou is an old state,
> Its Mandate is new.[12]

This refers to King Wen. If you can put heart into your practice you would also be able to renew your state.'

The Duke sent Pi Chan to ask about the well-field system.

'Your prince,' said Mencius, 'is going to practise benevolent government and has chosen you for this mission. You must do your best. Benevolent government must begin with land demarcation. When boundaries are not properly drawn, the division of land according to the well-field system and the yield of grain used for paying officials cannot be equitable. For this reason, despotic rulers and corrupt officials always neglect the boundaries. Once the boundaries are correctly fixed, there will be no difficulty in

"夫滕，壤地褊小，將為君子焉，將為野人焉。無君子，莫治野人；無野人，莫養君子。請野九一而助，國中什一使自賦。卿以下必有圭田，圭田五十畝；餘夫二十五畝。死徙無出鄉，鄉田同井，出入相友，守望相助，疾病相扶持，則百姓親睦。方里而井，井九百畝，其中為公田。八家皆私百畝，同養公田；公事畢，然後敢治私事，所以別野人也。此其大略也；若夫潤澤之，則在君與子矣。"

4. 有為神農之言者許行，自楚之滕，踵門而告文公曰："遠方之人

settling the distribution of land and the determination of emolument.

'T'eng is limited in territory. Nevertheless, there will be men in authority and there will be the common people. Without the former, there would be none to rule over the latter; without the latter, there would be none to support the former. I suggest that in the country the tax should be one in nine, using the method of *chu*, but in the capital it should be one in ten, to be levied in kind. From Ministers downwards, every official should have fifty *mu* of land for sacrificial purposes. In ordinary households, every extra man is to be given another twenty-five *mu*. Neither in burying the dead, nor in changing his abode, does a man go beyond the confines of his village. If those who own land within each *ching*[13] befriend one another both at home and abroad, help each other to keep watch, and succour each other in illness, they will live in love and harmony. A *ching* is a piece of land measuring one *li* square, and each *ching* consists of 900 *mu*. Of these, the central plot of 100 *mu* belongs to the state, while the other eight plots of 100 *mu* each are held by eight families who share the duty of caring for the plot owned by the state. Only when they have done this duty do they dare turn to their own affairs. This is what sets the common people apart.

'This is a rough outline. As for embellishments, I leave them to your prince and yourself.'

[6] Ode 154.

[7] This passage is also found in I. A. 7.

[8] Ode 212.

[9] Although he said earlier on that they used the *ch'e* method. On this point cf. I. B. 5, 'Formerly, when King Wen ruled over Ch'i, tillers of land were taxed one part in nine; descendants of officials received hereditary emoluments.'

[10] These are phonetic glosses, being near homophones of the words glossed.

[11] For the importance of understanding human relationships, cf., for instance, IV. B. 19, 'Shun understood the way of things and had a keen insight into human relationships.' and III. A. 4.

[12] Ode 235.

[13] As can be seen from the sequel, when a piece of land is divided into nine parts, it looks like the Chinese graph *ching* 井. Hence the system is known as *ching*-fields. The common translation of the term as 'well-fields', being based on the accident that the word *ching* means 'a well', is somewhat misleading, but I have kept it as it has become the standard translation.

4. There was a man by the name of Hsü Hsing who preached the

聞君行仁政，願受一廛而爲氓。"

文公與之處。

其徒數十人，皆衣褐，捆屨，織席以爲食。

陳良之徒陳相與其弟辛負耒耜而自宋之滕，曰："聞君行聖人之政，是亦聖人也，願爲聖人氓。"

陳相見許行而大悅，盡棄其學而學焉。

陳相見孟子，道許行之言曰："滕君則誠賢君也；雖然，未聞道也。賢者與民並耕而食，饔飧而治。今也滕有倉廩府庫，則是厲民而以自養也，惡得賢？"

孟子曰："許子必種粟而後食乎？"

曰："然。"

"許子必織布然後衣乎？"

曰："否；許子衣褐。"

"許子冠乎？"

曰："冠。"

曰："奚冠？"

曰："冠素。"

曰："自織之與？"

曰："否；以粟易之。"

曰："許子奚爲不自織？"

曰："害於耕。"

曰："許子以釜甑爨，以鐵耕乎？"

曰："然。"

teachings of Shen Nung.[14] He came to T'eng from Ch'u, went up to the gate and told Duke Wen, 'I, a man from distant parts, have heard that you, my lord, practise benevolent government. I wish to be given a place to live and become one of your subjects.'

The Duke gave him a place.

His followers, numbering several score, all wore unwoven hemp, and lived by making sandals and mats.

Ch'en Hsiang and his brother Hsin, both followers of Ch'en Liang, came to T'eng from Sung, carrying ploughs on their backs. 'We have heard,' said they, 'that you, my lord, practise the government of the sages. In that case you must yourself be a sage. We wish to be the subjects of a sage.'

Ch'en Hsiang met Hsü Hsing and was delighted with his teachings, so he abjured what he had learned before and became a follower of Hsü Hsing.

Ch'en Hsiang saw Mencius and cited the words of Hsü Hsing. 'The prince of T'eng is a truly good and wise ruler. However, he has never been taught the Way. To earn his keep a good and wise ruler shares the work of tilling the land with his people. He rules while cooking his own meals. Now T'eng has granaries and treasuries. This is for the prince to inflict hardship on the people in order to keep himself. How can he be a good and wise prince?'

'Does Hsü Tzu only eat grain he has grown himself?' asked Mencius.

'Yes.'

'Does Hsü Tzu only wear cloth he has woven himself?'

'No. He wears unwoven hemp.'

'Does Hsü Tzu wear a cap?'

'Yes.'

'What kind of cap does he wear?'

'Plain raw silk.'

'Does he weave it himself?'

'No. He trades grain for it.'

'Why does Hsü Tzu not weave it himself?'

'Because it interferes with his work in the fields.'

'Does Hsü Tzu use an iron pot and an earthenware steamer for cooking rice and iron implements for ploughing the fields?

'Yes.'

"自爲之與？"

曰："否；以粟易之。"

"以粟易械器者，不爲厲陶冶；陶冶亦以其械器易粟者，豈爲厲農夫哉？且許子何不爲陶冶，舍皆取諸其宮中而用之？何爲紛紛然與百工交易？何許子之不憚煩？"

曰："百工之事固不可耕且爲也。"

"然則治天下獨可耕且爲與？有大人之事，有小人之事。且一人之身，而百工之所爲備，如必自爲而後用之，是率天下而路也。故曰，或勞心，或勞力；勞心者治人，勞力者治於人；治於人者食人，治人者食於人，天下之通義也。

"當堯之時，天下猶未平，洪水橫流，氾濫於天下，草木暢茂，禽獸繁殖，五穀不登，禽獸偪人，獸蹄鳥跡之道交於中國。堯獨憂之，舉舜而敷治焉。舜使益掌火，益烈山澤而焚之，禽獸逃匿。禹疏九河，瀹濟漯而注諸海，決汝漢，排淮泗而注之江，然後中國可得而食也。當是時也，禹八年於外，三過其門而不入，雖欲耕，得乎？

"后稷教民稼穡，樹藝五穀；五穀熟而民人育。人之有道也，飽食、煖衣、逸居而無教，則近於禽獸。聖人有憂之，使契爲司徒，教以人倫，——父子有親，君臣有義，夫婦有別，長幼有敍，朋友有信。放勳曰：'勞之來之，匡之直之，輔之翼之，使自得之，又從而振德之。'聖人之憂民如此，而暇耕乎？

'Does he make them himself?'

'No. He trades grain for them.'

'To trade grain for implements is not to inflict hardship on the potter and the blacksmith. The potter and the blacksmith, for their part, also trade their wares for grain. In doing this, surely they are not inflicting hardship on the farmer either. Why does Hsü Tzu not be a potter and a blacksmith as well so that he can get everything he needs from his own house? Why does he indulge in such multifarious trading with men who practise the hundred crafts? Why does Hsü Tzu go to so much bother?'

'It is naturally impossible to combine the work of tilling the land with that of a hundred different crafts.'

'Now, is ruling the Empire such an exception that it can be combined with the work of tilling the land? There are affairs of great men, and there are affairs of small men. Moreover, it is necessary for each man to use the products of all the hundred crafts. If everyone must make everything he uses, the Empire will be led along the path of incessant toil. Hence it is said, "There are those who use their minds and there are those who use their muscles. The former rule; the latter are ruled. Those who rule are supported by those who are ruled." This is a principle accepted by the whole Empire.

'In the time of Yao, the Empire was not yet settled. The Flood[15] still raged unchecked, inundating the Empire; plants grew thickly; birds and beasts multiplied; the five grains did not ripen; birds and beasts encroached upon men, and their trail criss-crossed even the Central Kingdoms. The lot fell on Yao to worry about this situation. He raised Shun to a position of authority to deal with it. Shun put Yi in charge of fire. Yi ringed off the mountains and valleys and set them alight, and the birds and beasts went into hiding. Yü dredged the Nine Rivers, cleared the courses of the Chi and the T'a to channel the water into the Sea, deepened the beds of the Ju and the Han, and raised the dykes of the Huai and the Ssu to empty them into the River. Only then were the people of the Central Kingdoms able to find food for themselves. During this time Yü spent eight years abroad and passed the door of his own house three times without entering. Even if he had wished to plough the fields, could he have done it?

　　"堯以不得舜爲己憂，舜以不得禹皐陶爲己憂。夫以百畝之不易爲己憂者，農夫也。分人以財謂之惠，敎人以善謂之忠，爲天下得人者謂之仁。是故以天下與人易，爲天下得人難。孔子曰："大哉堯之爲君！惟天爲大，惟堯則之，蕩蕩乎民無能名焉！君哉舜也！巍巍乎有天下而不與焉！" 堯舜之治天下，豈無所用其心哉？亦不用於耕耳。

　　"吾聞用夏變夷者，未聞變於夷者也。陳良，楚產也，悅周公、仲尼之道，北學於中國。北方之學者，未能或之先也。彼所謂豪傑之士也。子之兄弟事之數十年，師死而遂倍之！昔者孔子沒，三年之外，門人治任將歸，入揖於子貢，相嚮而哭，皆失聲，然後歸。子貢反，築室於場，獨居三年，然後歸。他日，子夏、子張、子游以有若似聖人，欲以所事孔子事之，強曾子。曾子曰："不可；江漢以濯之，秋陽以暴之，皜皜乎不可尚已。" 今也南蠻鴃舌之人，非先王之道，子倍子之師而學之，亦異於曾子矣。吾聞出於幽谷遷于喬木者，未聞下喬木而入于幽谷者。魯頌曰："戎狄是膺，荊舒是懲。" 周公方且膺之，子是之學，亦爲不善變矣。"

'Hou Chi taught the people how to farm and grow the five kinds of grain. When these ripened, the people multiplied. This is the way of the common people: once they have a full belly and warm clothes on their back they degenerate to the level of animals if they are allowed to lead idle lives, without education and discipline. This gave the sage King further cause for concern, and so he appointed Hsieh as the Minister of Education whose duty was to teach the people human relationships: love between father and son, duty between ruler and subject, distinction between husband and wife, precedence of the old over the young, and faith between friends. Fang Hsün[16] said,

> Encourage them in their toil,
> Put them on the right path,
> Aid them and help them,
> Make them happy in their station,
> And by bountiful acts further relieve them of hardship.

The Sage worried to this extent about the affairs of the people. How could he have leisure to plough the fields? Yao's only worry was that he should fail to find someone like Shun, and Shun's only worry was that he should fail to find someone like Yü and Kao Yao. He who worries about his plot of a hundred *mu* not being well cultivated is a mere farmer.

'To share one's wealth with others is generosity; to teach others to be good is conscientiousness; to find the right man for the Empire is benevolence. Hence it is easier to give the Empire away than to find the right man for it.

'Confucius said, "Great indeed was Yao as a ruler! It is Heaven that is great, and it was Yao who modelled himself upon it. He was so boundless that the people were not able to put a name to his virtues. What a ruler Shun was! He was so lofty that while in possession of the Empire he held aloof from it."[17]

'It is not true that in ruling the Empire Yao and Shun did not have to use their minds. Only they did not use their minds on ploughing the fields.

'I have heard of the Chinese converting barbarians to their ways, but not of their being converted to barbarian ways. Ch'en Liang was a native of Ch'u. Being delighted with the way of the Duke of

"從許子之道，則市賈不貳，國中無偽；雖使五尺之童適市，莫之或欺。布帛長短同，則賈相若；麻縷絲絮輕重同，則賈相若；五穀多寡同，則賈相若；屨大小同，則賈相若。"

曰："夫物之不齊，物之情也；或相倍蓰，或相什百，或相千萬。子比而同之，是亂天下也。巨屨小屨同賈，人豈為之哉？從許子之道，相率而為偽者也，惡能治國家？"

Chou and Confucius, he came north to study in the Central Kingdoms. Even the scholars in the north could not surpass him in any way. He was what one would call an outstanding scholar. You and your brother studied under him for scores of years, and now that your teacher is dead, you turn your back on him.

'When Confucius died and the three-year mourning period had elapsed, his disciples packed their bags and prepared to go home. They went in and bowed to Tzu-kung and facing one another they wept until they lost their voices before setting out for home. Tzu-kung went back to build a hut in the burial grounds and remained there on his own for another three years before going home. One day, Tzu-hsia, Tzu-chang and Tzu-yu wanted to serve Yu Jo as they had served Confucius because of his resemblance to the Sage. They tried to force Tseng Tzu to join them, but Tseng Tzu said, "That will not do. Washed by the River and the river Han, bleached by the autumn sun, so immaculate was he that his whiteness could not be surpassed."

'Now you turn your back on the way of your teacher in order to follow the southern barbarian with the twittering tongue, who condemns the way of the Former Kings. You are indeed different from Tseng Tzu. I have heard of coming out of the dark ravine and going up to settle on a tall tree, but not of forsaking the tall tree to go down into the dark ravine. The *Lu sung* says,

> It was the barbarians that he attacked;
> It was Ching and Shu that he punished.[18]

It is these people the Duke of Chou was going to punish and you want to learn from them. That is not a change for the better, is it?'

'If we follow the way of Hsü Tzu there will only be one price in the market, and dishonesty will disappear from the capital. Even if you send a mere boy to the market, no one will take advantage of him. For equal lengths of cloth or silk, for equal weights of hemp, flax or raw silk, and for equal measures of the five grains, the price will be the same; for shoes of the same size, the price will also be the same.'

'That things are unequal is part of their nature. Some are worth twice or five times, ten or a hundred times, even a thousand and

5. 墨者夷之因徐辟而求見孟子。孟子曰："吾固願見，今吾尚病，病愈，我且往見，夷子不來！"

他日，又求見孟子。孟子曰："吾今則可以見矣。不直，則道不見；我且直之。吾聞夷子墨者，墨之治喪也，以薄爲其道也；夷子思以易天下，豈以爲非是而不貴也；然而夷子葬其親厚，則是以所賤事親也。"

徐子以告夷子。

夷子曰："儒者之道古之人若保赤子，此言何謂也？之則以爲愛無差等，施由親始。"

徐子以告孟子。

孟子曰："夫夷子信以爲[1]人之親其兄之子爲若親其鄰之赤子乎？彼有取爾也。赤子匍匐將入井，非赤子之罪也。且天之生物也，使之一本，而夷子二本故也。蓋上世嘗有不葬其親者，其親死，則舉而委之於壑。他日過之，狐狸食之，蠅蚋姑嘬之。其顙有泚，睨而不視。夫泚也，非爲人泚，中心達於面目，蓋歸反虆梩而掩之。掩之誠是也，則孝子仁人之掩其親，亦必有道矣。"

徐子以告夷子。夷子憮然爲間曰："命之矣。"

[1] 按此 '爲' 字與下 '爲' 字重複，疑爲後人誤增。

ten thousand times, more than others. If you reduce them to the same level, it will only bring confusion to the Empire. If a roughly finished shoe sells at the same price as a finely finished one, who would make the latter? If we follow the way of Hsü Tzu, we will be showing one another the way to being deceitful. How can one govern a state in this way?'

[14] The legendary Emperor credited with the invention of agriculture.
[15] Cf. p. 129 and Appendix 4.
[16] i.e., Yao.
[17] Cf. the *Analects of Confucius*, VIII. 18, 19.
[18] Ode 300.

5. Yi Chih, a Mohist, sought to meet Mencius through the good offices of Hsü Pi. 'I wish to see him too,' said Mencius, 'but at the moment I am not well. When I get better, I shall go to see him. There is no need for him to come here.'

Another day, he sought to see Mencius again. Mencius said, 'Now I can see him. If one does not put others right, one cannot hold the Way up for everyone to see. I shall put him right. I have heard that Yi Tzu is a Mohist. In funerals, the Mohists follow the way of frugality. Since Yi Tzu wishes to convert the Empire to frugality, it must be because he thinks it the only honourable way. But then Yi Tzu gave his parents lavish burials. In so doing, he treated his parents in a manner he did not esteem.'

Hsü Tzu reported this to Yi Tzu.

'The Confucians,' said Yi Tzu, 'praised the ancient rulers for acting "as if they were tending a new-born babe."[19] What does this saying mean? In my opinion, it means that there should be no gradations in love, though the practice of it begins with one's parents.'

Hsü Tzu reported this to Mencius.

'Does Yi Tzu truly believe,' said Mencius, 'that a man loves his brother's son no more than his neighbour's new-born babe? He is singling out a special feature in a certain case: when the new-born babe creeps towards a well it is not its fault.[20] Moreover, when Heaven produces things, it gives them a single basis, yet Yi Tzu tries to give them a dual one.[21] This accounts for his belief.

'Presumably there must have been cases in ancient times of

people not burying their parents. When the parents died, they were thrown in the gullies. Then one day the sons passed the place and there lay the bodies, eaten by foxes and sucked by flies. A sweat broke out on their brows, and they could not bear to look. The sweating was not put on for others to see. It was an outward expression of their innermost heart. They went home for baskets and spades. If it was truly right for them to bury the remains of their parents, then it must also be right for all dutiful sons and benevolent men to do likewise.'

Hsü Tzu repeated this to Yi Tzu who looked lost for quite a while and replied, 'I have taken his point.'

[19] This saying is to be found in the *K'ang kao* chapter of the *Book of History*. (*Shu ching*, 14. 6b).

[20] This seems to be a reference to the example given in II. A. 6 of a new-born babe creeping towards a well.

[21] By a dual basis, Mencius is presumably referring to the incompatibility between the denial of gradations of love and the insistence on its practice beginning with one's parents.

滕文公章句下

1.　陳代曰：“不見諸侯，宜若小然；今一見之，大則以王，小則以霸。且志曰：‘枉尺而直尋。’宜若可爲也。”

　　孟子曰：“昔齊景公田，招虞人以旌，不至，將殺之，志士不忘在溝壑，勇士不忘喪其元。孔子奚取焉？取非其招不往也。如不待其招而往何哉？且夫枉尺而直尋者，以利言也。如以利，則枉尋直尺而利，亦可爲與？昔者趙簡子使王良與嬖奚乘，終日而不獲一禽。嬖奚反命曰：‘天下之賤工也。’或以告王良。良曰：‘請復之。’強而後可，一朝而獲十禽。嬖奚反命曰：‘天下之良工也。’簡子曰：‘我使掌與女乘。’謂王良。良不可，曰：‘吾爲之範我馳驅，終日不獲一；爲之詭遇，一朝而獲十。詩云：“不失其馳，舍矢如破。”我不貫與小人乘，請辭。’御者且羞與射者比；比而得禽獸，雖若丘陵，弗爲也。如枉道而從彼何也？且子過矣：枉己者，未有能直人者也。”

BOOK III · PART B

1. Ch'en Tai said, 'When you refused even to see them, the feudal lords naturally appeared insignificant to you. Now that you have seen them, they are either kings or, at least, leaders of the feudal lords. Moreover, it is said in the *Records*, "Bend the foot in order to straighten the yard." That seems worth doing.'

'Once,' said Mencius, 'Duke Ching of Ch'i went hunting and summoned his gamekeeper with a pennon.[1] The gamekeeper did not come, and the Duke was going to have him put to death. "A man whose mind is set on high ideals never forgets that he may end in a ditch; a man of valour never forgets that he may forfeit his head." What was it that Confucius found praiseworthy in the gamekeeper? His refusal to answer to a form of summons to which he was not entitled.[2] What can one do about those who go without even being summoned? Moreover, the saying "Bend the foot in order to straighten the yard" refers to profit. If it is for profit, I suppose one might just as well bend the yard to straighten the foot.

'Once, Viscount Chien of Chao sent Wang Liang to drive the chariot for his favourite, Hsi. Throughout the day they failed to catch one single bird. Hsi reported to his master, "He is the worst charioteer in the world." Someone told Wang Liang of this. Liang asked, "May I have another chance?" It was with difficulty that Hsi was persuaded, but in one morning they caught ten birds. Hsi reported to his master, "He is the best charioteer in the world." "I shall make him drive for you," said Viscount Chien. He asked Wang Liang, but Wang Liang refused. "I drove for him according to the proper rules," said he, "and throughout the day we did not catch a single bird. Then I used underhand methods, and we caught ten birds in one morning. The *Odes* say,

> He never failed to drive correctly,
> And his arrows went straight for the target.[3]

I am not used to driving for small men. May I be excused?"

'Even a charioteer is ashamed to be in league with an archer. When doing so means catching enough birds to pile up like a mountain, he would still rather not do it. What can one do about

2.　景春曰："公孫衍、張儀豈不誠大丈夫哉？一怒而諸侯懼，安居而天下熄。"

　　孟子曰："是焉得為大丈夫乎？子未學禮乎？丈夫之冠也，父命之；女子之嫁也，母命之，往送之門，戒之曰：'往之女家，必敬必戒，無違夫子！' 以順為正者，妾婦之道也。居天下之廣居，立天下之正位，行天下之大道；得志，與民由之；不得志，獨行其道。富貴不能淫，貧賤不能移，威武不能屈，此之謂大丈夫。"

3.　周霄問曰："古之君子仕乎？"

　　孟子曰："仕。"

　　"傳曰：'孔子三月無君，則皇皇如也，出疆必載質。' 公明儀曰：'古之人三月無君，則弔。' 三月無君則弔，不以急乎？"

　　曰："士之失位也，猶諸侯之失國家也。禮曰：'諸侯耕助以供粢盛；夫人蠶繅，以為衣服。犧牲不成，粢盛不絜，衣服不備，不敢

those who bend the Way in order to please others? You are further mistaken. There has never been a man who could straighten others by bending himself.'

[1] For this incident see the *Tso chuan*, Duke Chao 20. Cf. p. 217 where the appropriate means of summons are explained.

[2] Cf. V. B. 7.

[3] Ode 179.

2. Ching Ch'un said, 'Are not Kung-sun Yen and Chang Yi great men? As soon as they show their wrath the feudal lords tremble with fear, and when they are still the Empire is spared the conflagration of war.'

'How can they be thought great men?' said Mencius. 'Have you never studied the rites? When a man comes of age his father gives him advice.[4] When a girl marries, her mother gives her advice, and accompanies her to the door with these cautionary words, "When you go to your new home, you must be respectful and circumspect. Do not disobey your husband." It is the way of a wife or concubine to consider obedience and docility the norm.

'A man lives in the spacious dwelling, occupies the proper position, and goes along the highway of the Empire.[5] When he achieves his ambition he shares these with the people; when he fails to do so he practises the Way alone. He cannot be led into excesses when wealthy and honoured or deflected from his purpose when poor and obscure, nor can he be made to bow before superior force. This is what I would call a great man.'

[4] Judging by the context, the advice given by the father should be quoted as a contrast to that given by the mother. Otherwise, there seems little point in just mentioning the father's advice. The present text is probably defective.

[5] Cf. 'Benevolence is man's peaceful abode and rightness his proper path' (IV. A. 10).

3. Chou Hsiao asked, 'Did the gentlemen in ancient times take office?'

'Yes,' said Mencius.

'The *Records* say, "When Confucius was not in the service of a lord for three months, he became agitated. When he left for another state, he always took with him a token of allegiance for the first audience." Kung-ming Yi said, "In ancient times when a

以祭。惟士無田，則亦不祭。’牲殺器皿、衣服不備，不敢以祭，則不敢以宴，亦不足弔乎？”

“出疆必載質，何也？”

曰：“士之仕也，猶農夫之耕也；農夫豈爲出疆舍其耒耜哉？”

曰：“晉國亦仕國也，未嘗聞仕如此其急。仕如此其急也，君子之難仕，何也？”

曰：“丈夫生而願爲之有室，女子生而願爲之有家；父母之心，人皆有之。不待父母之命、媒妁之言，鑽穴隙相窺，踰牆相從，則父母國人皆賤之。古之人未嘗不欲仕也，又惡不由其道。不由其道而往者，與 [1] 鑽穴隙之類也。”

[1] ‘與’讀爲‘舉’。

4. 彭更問曰：“後車數十乘，從者數百人，以傳食於諸侯，不以泰乎？”

孟子曰：“非其道，則一簞食不可受於人；如其道，則舜受堯之天下，不以爲泰——子以爲泰乎？”

曰：“否；士無事而食，不可也。”

曰：“子不通功易事，以羨補不足，則農有餘粟，女有餘布；子

man was not in the service of a lord for three months he was offered condolences." 'Does this not show an unseemly haste?'

'A Gentleman losing his position is like a feudal lord losing his state. The *Rites* say, "A feudal lord takes part in the ploughing to supply the grain for sacrificial offerings. His wife takes part in sericulture to provide the material for sacrificial dresses. When the sacrificial animals are not fat, the grain not clean and the items of dress not ready, he dare not perform the sacrifice. In the case of a Gentleman, if he has no land, he does not offer sacrifices" If when the vessels used for killing the animals and the items of dress are not ready one dare not offer sacrifices, then is it not serious enough for condolences to be offered when one dare not hold banquets?'

'Why did Confucius always take with him a token of allegiance when he left for another state?'

'A Gentleman takes office as a farmer cultivates his land. Does a farmer leave his farming tools behind just because he is leaving for another state?'

'People here in Chin take office as in any other state, but I have never heard of such haste. If taking office is such an urgent matter, why does a Gentleman find it so hard to take office?'

'When a man is born his parents wish that he may one day find a wife, and when a woman is born they wish that she may find a husband. Every parent feels like this. But those who bore holes in the wall to peep at one another, and climb over it to meet illicitly, waiting for neither the command of parents nor the good offices of a go-between, are despised by parents and fellow-countrymen alike. In ancient times men were indeed eager to take office, but they disliked seeking it by dishonourable means, for all those who do so are no different from the men and women who bore holes in the wall.'

4. P'eng Keng asked, 'Is it not excessive to travel with a retinue of hundreds of followers in scores of chariots, and to live off one feudal lord after another?'

'If it is not in accordance with the Way,' answered Mencius, 'one should not accept even one basketful of rice from another person. On the other hand, Shun accepted the Empire from Yao without considering it excessive, when it was in accordance with

如通之，則梓匠輪輿皆得食於子。於此有人焉，入則孝，出則悌，守
先王之道，以待後之學者，而不得食於子；子何尊梓匠輪輿而輕爲仁
義者哉？"

曰："梓匠輪輿，其志將以求食也；君子之爲道也，其志亦將以
求食與？"

曰："子何以其志爲哉？其有功於子，可食而食之矣。且子食志
乎？食功乎？"

曰："食志。"

曰："有人於此，毀瓦畫墁，其志將以求食也，則子食之乎？"

曰："否。"

曰："然則子非食志也，食功也。"

5.　萬章問曰："宋，小國也；今將行仁政，齊楚惡而伐之，則如之
何？"

孟子曰："湯居亳，與葛爲鄰，葛伯放而不祀。湯使人問之曰：
'何爲不祀？'曰：'無以供犧牲也。'湯使遺之牛羊。葛伯食之，
又不以祀。湯又使人問之曰：'何爲不祀？'曰：'無以供粢盛也。'湯
使亳衆往爲之耕，老弱饋食。葛伯率其民，要其有酒食黍稻者奪之，
不授者殺之。有童子以黍肉餉，殺而奪之。書曰：'葛伯仇餉。'此
之謂也。爲其殺是童子而征之，四海之內皆曰：'非富天下也，爲匹
夫匹婦復讎也。''湯始征，自葛載，'十一征而無敵於天下。東面
而征，西夷怨；南面而征，北狄怨，曰：'奚爲後我？'民之望之，

the Way. Or perhaps you consider even that excessive?'

'No. But it is not right for a Gentleman not to earn his keep.'

'If people cannot trade the surplus of the fruits of their labour to satisfy one another's needs, then the farmer will be left with surplus grain and the women with surplus cloth. If things are exchanged, you can feed the carpenter and the carriage-maker. Here is a man. He is obedient to his parents at home and respectful to his elders abroad and acts as custodian of the way of the Former Kings for the benefit of future students. In spite of that, you say he ought not to be fed. Why do you place more value on the carpenter and the carriage-maker than on a man who practises morality?'

'It is the intention of the carpenter and the carriage-maker to make a living. When a Gentleman pursues the Way, is it also his intention to make a living?'

'What has intention got to do with it? If he does good work for you then you ought to feed him whenever possible. Moreover, do you feed people on account of their intentions or on account of their work?'

'Their intentions.'

'Here is a man who makes wild movements with his trowel, ruining the tiles. Would you feed him because his intention is to make a living?'

'No.'

'Then you feed people on account of their work, not on account of their intentions.'

5. Wan Chang asked, 'If Sung, a small state, were to practise Kingly government and be attacked by Ch'i and Ch'u for doing so, what could be done about it?'

'When T'ang was in Po,' answered Mencius, 'his territory adjoined the state of Ke. The Earl of Ke was a wilful man who neglected his sacrificial duties. T'ang sent someone to ask, "Why do you not offer sacrifices?" "We have no suitable animals." T'ang had gifts of oxen and sheep sent to the Earl of Ke, but he used them for food and continued to neglect his sacrificial duties. T'ang once again sent someone to ask, "Why do you not offer sacrifices?" "We have no suitable grain." T'ang sent the people of Po to help

若大旱之望雨也。歸市者弗止，芸者不變，誅其君，弔其民，如時雨
降。民大悅。書曰：'徯我后，后來其無罰！' '有攸¹不惟臣，東
征，綏厥士女，篚厥玄黃，紹我周王見休，惟臣附于大邑周。' 其君
子實玄黃于篚以迎其君子，其小人簞食壺漿以迎其小人；救民於水火
之中，取其殘而已矣。太誓曰：'我武惟揚，侵于之疆，則取于殘，
殺伐用張，于湯有光。' 不行王政云爾；苟行王政，四海之內皆舉首
而望之，欲以為君；齊楚雖大，何畏焉？"

¹ '攸' 為國名，說見陳夢家《殷虛卜辭綜述》頁306。'有' 乃語首助詞。'攸' 之
稱 '有攸' 猶 '苗' 之稱 '有苗'。

in the ploughing and also sent the aged and young with gifts of food. The Earl of Ke led his people out and waylaid those who were bringing wine, food, millet and rice, trying to take these things from them by force. Those who resisted were killed. A boy bearing millet and meat was killed and the food taken. The *Book of History* says,

> The Earl of Ke treated those who brought food as enemies.

That is the incident to which this refers. When an army was sent to punish Ke for killing the boy, the whole Empire said, "This is not coveting the Empire but avenging common men and common women."

> T'ang began his punitive expeditions with Ke.[6]

In eleven expeditions he became matchless in the Empire. When he marched on the east, the western barbarians complained, and when he marched on the south, the northern barbarians complained. They all said, "Why does he not come to us first?"[7] The people longed for his coming as they longed for rain in time of severe drought. Those who were going to market did not stop; those who were weeding went on weeding. He punished the rulers and comforted the people, like a fall of timely rain, and the people rejoiced greatly. The *Book of History* says,

> We await our Lord. When he comes we will suffer no more.

> The state of Yu did not submit. The King went east to punish it, bringing peace to men and women. They put bundles of black and yellow silk into baskets as gifts, seeking the honour of an audience with the King of Chou, and declared themselves subjects of the great state of Chou.[8]

The gentlemen filled baskets with black and yellow silk to bid the gentlemen welcome; the common people brought baskets of food and bottles of drink to bid the common people welcome. The King of Chou rescued the people from water and fire and took captive only their cruel masters. The *T'ai shih* says,

> We show our military might and attack the territory of Yü, taking captive their cruel rulers. Our punitive acts are glorious. In this we surpass even T'ang.[9]

6. 孟子謂戴不勝曰：“子欲子之王之善與？我明告子。有楚大夫於此，欲其子之齊語也，則使齊人傅諸？使楚人傅諸？”

曰：“使齊人傅之。”

曰：“一齊人傅之，衆楚人咻之，雖日撻而求其齊也，不可得矣；引而置之莊嶽之閒數年，雖日撻而求其楚，亦不可得矣。子謂薛居州，善士也，使之居於王所。在於王所者，長幼卑尊皆薛居州也，王誰與爲不善？在王所者，長幼卑尊皆非薛居州也，王誰與爲善？一薛居州，獨如宋王何？”

7. 公孫丑問曰：“不見諸侯何義？”

孟子曰：“古者不爲臣不見。段干木踰垣而辟之，泄柳閉門而不納，是皆已甚；迫，斯可以見矣。陽貨欲見孔子而惡無禮，大夫有賜於士，不得受於其家，則往拜其門。陽貨矙孔子之亡也，而饋孔子蒸

It is all a matter of failing to practise Kingly government. If you should practise Kingly government, all within the Four Seas would raise their heads to watch for your coming, desiring you as their ruler. Ch'i and Ch'u may be big in size, but what is there to be afraid of?'

[6]For this quotation and the whole of the passage following, see the parallel passage in I. B. 11.

[7]Cf. also VII. B. 4.

[8]This quotation about the state of Yu is presumably also from a lost chapter of the *Book of History*, though it has been incorporated into the spurious *Wu ch'eng* of the present text. See *Shu ching*, II. 23b.

[9]From the lost *T'ai shih*, though in the present *Book of History*, this has again been incorporated into the spurious chapter bearing the same name. See ibid., II. 10a.

6. Mencius said to Tai Pu-sheng, 'Do you wish your King[10] to be good? I shall speak to you plainly. Suppose a Counsellor of Ch'u wished his son to speak the language of Ch'i. Would he have a man from Ch'i to tutor his son? Or would he have a man from Ch'u?'

'He would have a man from Ch'i to tutor his son.'

'With one man from Ch'i tutoring the boy and a host of Ch'u men chattering around him, even though you caned him every day to make him speak Ch'i, you would not succeed. Take him away to some district like Chuang and Yüeh[11] for a few years, then even if you caned him every day to make him speak Ch'u, you would not succeed. You have placed Hsüeh Chü-chou near the King because you think him a good man. If everyone around the King, old or young, high or low, is a Hsüeh Chü-chou, then who will help the King to do evil? But if no one around the King is a Hsüeh Chü-chou, then who will help the King to do good? What difference can one Hsüeh Chü-chou make to the King of Sung?'

[10]This is Yen, the King of Sung.

[11]It is possible that these are names of streets in Ch'i.

7. Kung-sun Ch'ou asked, 'What is the significance of your not trying to see the feudal lords?'

'In ancient times,' said Mencius, 'one did not try to see a feudal lord unless one held office under him. Tuan-kan Mu climbed over a wall to avoid a meeting;[12] Hsieh Liu bolted his door and refused

豚；孔子亦矙其亡也，而往拜之。當是時，陽貨先，豈得不見？曾子曰：'脅肩諂笑，病于夏畦。' 子路曰：'未同而言，觀其色赧赧然，非由之所知也。' 由是觀之，則君子之所養，可知已矣。"

8.　戴盈之曰："什一，去關市之征，今茲未能，請輕之，以待來年，然後已，何如？"

孟子曰："今有人日攘其鄰之雞者，或告之曰：'是非君子之道。' 曰：'請損之，月攘一雞，以待來年，然後已。'——如知其非義，斯速已矣，何待來年？"

9.　公都子曰："外人皆稱夫子好辯，敢問何也？"

孟子曰："予豈好辯哉？予不得已也。天下之生久矣，一治一亂。當堯之時，水逆行，氾濫於中國，蛇龍居之，民無所定；下者爲巢，上者爲營窟。 書曰：'洚水警余。' 洚水者，洪水也。使禹治之。禹掘地而注之海，驅蛇龍而放之菹；水由地中行，江、淮、河、漢是也。險阻既遠，鳥獸之害人者消，然後人得平土而居之。

admittance.[13] Both went too far. When forced, one may see them.

'Yang Huo wanted to see Confucius, but disliked acting in a manner contrary to the rites. When a Counsellor made a gift to a Gentleman, the Gentleman, if he was not at home to receive it, had to go to the Counsellor's home to offer his thanks. Yang Huo waited until Confucius was out before presenting him with a steamed piglet. But Confucius also waited until Yang Huo went out before going to offer his thanks.[14] At that time if Yang Huo had taken the initiative in showing courtesy to Confucius, how could Confucius have refused to see him? Tseng Tzu said, "It is more fatiguing to shrug one's shoulders and smile ingratiatingly than to work on a vegetable plot in the summer." Tzu-lu said, "To concur while not in agreement and to show this by blushing is quite beyond my understanding." From this it is not difficult to see what it is a gentleman cultivates in himself.'

[12] with the lord of Wei.
[13] to the Duke of Lu.
[14] Cf. the *Analects of Confucius*, XVII. I.

8. Tai Ying-chih said, 'We are unable in the present year to change over to a tax of one in ten and to abolish custom and market duties. What would you think if we were to make some reductions and wait till next year before putting the change fully into effect?'

'Here is a man,' said Mencius, 'who appropriates one of his neighbour's chickens every day. Someone tells him, "This is not how a gentleman behaves." He answers, "May I reduce it to one chicken every month and wait until next year to stop altogether?"'

'When one realizes that something is morally wrong, one should stop it as soon as possible. Why wait for next year?'

9. Kung-tu Tzu said, 'Outsiders all say that you, Master, are fond of disputation. May I ask why?'

'I am not fond of disputation,' answered Mencius. 'I have no alternative. The world has existed for a long time, now in peace, now in disorder. In the time of Yao, the water reversed its natural course, flooding the central regions, and the reptiles made their homes there, depriving the people of a settled life. In low-lying regions, people lived in nests; in high regions, they lived in caves.

"堯舜既沒，聖人之道衰，暴君代作，壞宮室以爲汙池，民無所安息；棄田以爲園囿，使民不得衣食。邪說暴行又作，園囿、汙池、沛澤多而禽獸至。及紂之身，天下又大亂。周公相武王誅紂，伐奄三年討其君，驅飛廉於海隅而戮之，滅國者五十，驅虎、豹、犀、象而遠之，天下大悅。書曰：'丕顯哉，文王謨！丕承哉，武王烈！佑啓我後人，咸以正無缺。'

"世衰道微，邪說暴行有作，臣弑其君者有之，子弑其父者有之。孔子懼，作春秋。春秋，天子之事也；是故孔子曰：'知我者其惟春秋乎！罪我者其惟春秋乎！'

"聖王不作，諸侯放恣，處士橫議，楊朱、墨翟之言盈天下。天下之言不歸楊，則歸墨。楊氏爲我，是無君也；墨氏兼愛，是無父也。無父無君，是禽獸也。公明儀曰：'庖有肥肉，廄有肥馬；民有飢色，野有餓莩，此率獸而食人也。'楊墨之道不息，孔子之道不著，是邪說誣民，充塞仁義也。仁義充塞，則率獸食人，人將相食。吾爲此懼，閑先聖之道，距楊墨，放淫辭，邪說者不得作。作於其心，害於其事；作於其事，害於其政。聖人復起，不易吾言矣。

The *Book of History* says,

> The Deluge was a warning to us.[15]

By the "Deluge" was meant the "Flood". Yü was entrusted with the task of controlling it. He led the flood water into the seas by cutting channels for it in the ground, and drove the reptiles into grassy marshes. The water, flowing through the channels, formed the Yangtse, and Huai, the Yellow River and the Han. Obstacles receded and the birds and beasts harmful to men were annihilated. Only then were the people able to level the ground and live on it.

'After the death of Yao and Shun, the way of the Sages declined, and tyrants arose one after another. They pulled down houses in order to make ponds, and the people had nowhere to rest. They turned fields into parks, depriving the people of their livelihood. Moreover, heresies and violence arose. With the multiplication of parks, ponds and lakes, arrived birds and beasts. By the time of the tyrant Tchou, the Empire was again in great disorder. The Duke of Chou helped King Wu to punish Tchou. He waged war on Yen for three years and punished its ruler; he drove Fei Lien to the edge of the sea and executed him. He annexed fifty states. He drove tigers, leopards, rhinoceroses and elephants to remote parts, and the Empire rejoiced. The *Book of History* says,

> Lofty indeed were the plans of King Wen!
> Great indeed were the achievements of King Wu!
> Bless us and enlighten us, your descendants,
> So that we may act correctly and not fall into error.[16]

'When the world declined and the Way fell into obscurity, heresies and violence again arose. There were instances of regicides and patricides. Confucius was apprehensive and composed the *Spring and Autumn Annals*. Strictly speaking, this is the Emperor's prerogative. That is why Confucius said, "Those who understand me will do so through the *Spring and Autumn Annals*; those who condemn me will also do so because of the *Spring and Autumn Annals*."

'No sage kings have appeared since then. Feudal lords do as they please; people with no official position are uninhibited in the expression of their views,[17] and the words of Yang Chu and Mo Ti

"昔者禹抑洪水而天下平，周公兼夷狄，驅猛獸而百姓寧，孔子成春秋而亂臣賊子懼。詩云：'戎狄是膺，荆舒是懲，則莫我敢承。'無父無君，是周公所膺也。我亦欲正人心，息邪說，詎詖行，放淫辭，以承三聖者；豈好辯哉？予不得已也。能言距楊墨者，聖人之徒也。"

fill the Empire. The teachings current in the Empire are those of either the school of Yang or the school of Mo. Yang advocates everyone for himself, which amounts to a denial of one's prince; Mo advocates love without discrimination,[18] which amounts to a denial of one's father. To ignore one's father on the one hand, and one's prince on the other, is to be no different from the beasts. Kung-ming Yi said, "There is fat meat in your kitchen and there are well-fed horses in your stables, yet the people look hungry and in the outskirts of cities men drop dead from starvation. This is to show animals the way to devour men."[19] If the way of Yang and Mo does not subside and the way of Confucius is not proclaimed, the people will be deceived by heresies and the path of morality will be blocked. When the path of morality is blocked, then we show animals the way to devour men, and sooner or later it will come to men devouring men. Therefore, I am apprehensive. I wish to safeguard the way of the former sages against the onslaughts of Yang and Mo and to banish excessive views. Then there will be no way for advocates of heresies to arise. For what arises in the mind will interfere with policy, and what shows itself in policy will interfere with practice. Were there once more a sage, he would surely agree with what I have said.[20]

'In ancient times Yü controlled the Flood and brought peace to the Empire; the Duke of Chou subjugated the northern and southern barbarians, drove away the wild animals, and brought security to the people; Confucius completed the *Spring and Autumn Annals* and struck terror into the hearts of rebellious subjects and undutiful sons. The *Odes* say,

> It was the barbarians that he attacked.
> It was Ching and Shu that he punished.
> "There was none who dared stand up to me."[21]

The Duke of Chou wanted to punish those who ignored father and prince. I, too, wish to follow in the footsteps of the three sages in rectifying the hearts of men, laying heresies to rest, opposing extreme action, and banishing excessive views. I am not fond of disputation. I have no alternative. Whoever can, with words, combat Yang and Mo is a true disciple of the sages.'

10. 匡章曰：「陳仲子豈不誠廉士哉？居於陵，三日不食，耳無聞，目無見也。井上有李，螬食實者過半矣，匍匐往，將食之；三咽，然後耳有聞，目有見。」

孟子曰：「於齊國之士，吾必以仲子為巨擘焉。雖然，仲子惡能廉？充仲子之操，則蚓而後可者也。夫蚓，上食槁壤，下飲黃泉。仲子所居之室，伯夷之所築與？抑亦盜跖之所築與？所食之粟，伯夷之所樹與？抑亦盜跖之所樹與？是未可知也。」

曰：「是何傷哉？彼身織屨，妻辟纑，以易之也。」

曰：「仲子，齊之世家也，兄戴，蓋祿萬鍾；以兄之祿為不義之祿而不食也，以兄之室為不義之室而不居也，辟兄離母，處於於陵。他日歸，則有饋其兄生鵝者，己頻顣曰：『惡用是鶃鶃者為哉？』他日，其母殺是鵝也，與之食之。其兄自外至，曰：『是鶃鶃之肉也。』出而哇之。以母則不食，以妻則食之；以兄之室則弗居，以於陵則居之，是尚為能充其類也乎？若仲子者，蚓而後充其操者也。」

[15]From a lost chapter.

[16]From a lost chapter but incorporated into the spurious *Chün ya* chapter (*Shu ching*, 19. 22a–b).

[17]Cf. IV. A. 22.

[18]Cf. VII. A. 26.

[19]This saying is also found in I. A. 14 though there it is not attributed to Kung-ming Yi.

[20]For these two sentences cf. II. A. 2.

[21]Ode 300.

10. K'uang Chang said, 'Is Ch'en Chung-tzu not truly a man of scruples? When he was in Wu Ling, he went without food for three days and as a result could neither hear with his ears nor see with his eyes. By the well was a plum tree, more than half of whose plums were worm-eaten. He crept up, took one and ate it. Only after three mouthfuls was he able to hear with his ears and see with his eyes.'

'I count Chung-tzu as the finest among Gentlemen in the state of Ch'i,' said Mencius. 'Even so, how can he pass for a man of scruples? Pushed to its utmost limits, his way of life would only be possible for an earthworm which eats the dry earth above and drinks from the yellow spring below. Was the house where Chung-tzu lived built by Po Yi? Or was it built by the Bandit Chih? Was the millet he ate grown by Po Yi? Or was it grown by the Bandit Chih? The answer cannot be known.'

'What does it matter? He himself made sandals and his wife made hemp and silk thread to barter for these things.'

'Chung-tzu came from an old family. His elder brother Tai had an income of ten thousand bushels, but he considered his brother's income ill-gotten and refused to benefit from it, and he considered his brother's house ill-gotten and refused to live in it. He lived in Wu Ling apart from his brother and mother. One day when he came home for a visit and found that his brother had been given a present of a live goose, he knitted his brow and said, "What does one want this honking creature for?" Another day, his mother killed the goose and gave it to him to eat. His brother came home and said, "This is the meat of that honking creature." He went out and vomited it all out. He ate what his wife provided but not what his mother provided. He lived in Wu Ling but not in his brother's house. Did he think that he had succeeded in pushing his principle

to the utmost limits? Pushed to the utmost limits his way of life would only be possible if he were an earthworm.'

離婁章句上

1.　孟子曰：“離婁之明、公輸子之巧，不以規矩，不能成方員；師曠之聰，不以六律，不能正五音；堯舜之道，不以仁政，不能平治天下。今有仁心仁聞而民不被其澤，不可法於後世者，不行先王之道也。故曰，徒善不足以爲政，徒法不能以自行。詩云，‘不愆不忘，率由舊章。’遵先王之法而過者，未之有也。聖人既竭目力焉，繼之以規矩準繩，以爲方員平直，不可勝用也；既竭耳力焉，繼之以六律正五音，不可勝用也；既竭心思焉，繼之以不忍人之政，而仁覆天下矣。故曰：‘爲高必因丘陵，爲下必因川澤。’爲政不因先王之道，可謂智乎？是以惟仁者宜在高位。不仁而在高位，是播其惡於衆也。上無道揆也，下無法守也，朝不信道，工不信度，君子犯義，小人犯刑，國之所存者幸也。故曰：‘城郭不完，兵甲不多，非國之災也；田野不辟，貨財不聚，非國之害也。上無禮，下無學，賊民興，喪無日矣。’詩曰：‘天之方蹶，無然泄泄。’泄泄猶沓沓也。事君無義，進退無禮，言則非先王之道者，猶沓沓也。故曰，責難於君謂之恭，陳善閉邪謂之敬，吾君不能謂之賊。”

BOOK IV · PART A

1. Mencius said, 'Even if you had the keen eyes of Li Lou and the skill of Kung-shu Tzu, you could not draw squares or circles without a carpenter's square or a pair of compasses; even if you had the acute ears of Shih K'uang, you could not adjust the pitch of the five notes correctly without the six pipes; even if you knew the way of Yao and Shun, you could not rule the Empire equitably except through benevolent government. Now there are some who, despite their benevolent hearts and reputations, succeed neither in benefiting the people by their benevolence nor in setting an example for posterity. This is because they do not practise the way of the Former Kings. Hence it is said,

> Goodness alone is not sufficient for government;
> The law unaided cannot make itself effective.

The *Odes* say,

> Do not swerve to one side, do not overlook anything;
> Follow established rules in everything you do.[1]

No one ever erred through following the example of the Former Kings.

'The sage, having taxed his eyes to their utmost capacity, went on to invent the compasses and the square, the level and the plumb-line, which can be used endlessly for the production of squares and circles, planes and straight lines, and, having taxed his ears to their utmost capacity, he went on to invent the six pipes which can be used endlessly for setting the pitch of the five notes, and, having taxed his heart to its utmost capacity, he went on to practise government that tolerated no suffering, thus putting the whole Empire under the shelter of his benevolence. Hence it is said, "To build high one should always take advantage of existing hills, to dig deep one should always take advantage of existing rivers and marshes." Can one be deemed wise if, in governing the people, one fails to take advantage of the way of the Former Kings? Hence, only the benevolent man is fit to be in high position. For a cruel man to be in high position is for him to disseminate his wickedness among the

2.　孟子曰：「規矩、方員之至也；聖人、人倫之至也。欲爲君，盡
君道；欲爲臣，盡臣道。二者皆法堯舜而已矣。不以舜之所以事堯事
君，不敬其君者也；不以堯之所以治民治民，賊其民者也。孔子曰：
　‘道二，仁與不仁而已矣。’暴其民甚，則身弑國亡；不甚，則身危
國削，名之曰‘幽’‘厲’，雖孝子慈孫，百世不能改也。詩云：
　‘殷鑒不遠，在夏后之世。’此之謂也。」

people. When those above have no principles and those below have no laws, when countries have no faith in the Way and craftsmen have no faith in measures, when gentlemen offend against what is right and common people risk punishment, then it is good fortune indeed if a state survives. Hence it is said, "When the city walls are not intact and arms are not abundant, it is no disaster for a state. When waste land is not brought under cultivation and wealth is not accumulated, this, too, is no disaster for the state. But when those above ignore the rites, those below ignore learning, and lawless people arise, then the end of the state is at hand." The *Odes* say,

> Heaven is about to stir,
> Do not chatter so.[2]

"To chatter" is "to talk too much". To ignore dutifulness in serving one's ruler, to disregard the rites in accepting and relinquishing office, and yet to make calumnious attacks on the way of the Former Kings is what is meant by "talking too much". Hence it is said, "To take one's prince to task is respect; to discourse on the good and keep out heresies is reverence; to say 'My prince will never be capable of it' is to cripple him." '

[1]Ode 249.
[2]Ode 254.

2. Mencius said, 'The compasses and the carpenter's square are the culmination of squares and circles; the sage is the culmination of humanity. If one wishes to be a ruler, one must fulfil the duties proper to a ruler; if one wishes to be a subject, one must fulfil the duties proper to a subject. In both cases all one has to do is to model oneself on Yao and Shun. Not to serve one's prince in the way Shun served Yao is not to respect one's prince; not to govern the people in the way Yao governed his is to harm one's people. Confucius said, "There are two ways and two only: benevolence and cruelty." If a ruler ill-uses his people to an extreme degree, he will be murdered and his state annexed; if he does it to a lesser degree, his person will be in danger and his territory reduced. Such rulers will be given the posthumous names of "Yu" and "Li",[3] and even dutiful sons and grandsons will not be able to have them revoked in a hundred generations. The *Odes* say,

3. 孟子曰："三代之得天下也以仁，其失天下也以不仁。國之所以廢興存亡者亦然。天子不仁，不保四海；諸侯不仁，不保社稷；卿大夫不仁，不保宗廟；士庶人不仁，不保四體。今惡死亡而樂不仁，是由惡醉而強酒。"

4. 孟子曰："愛人不親，反其仁；治人不治，反其智；禮人不答，反其敬——行有不得者皆反求諸己，其身正而天下歸之。詩云：'永言配命，自求多福。'"

5. 孟子曰："人有恆言，皆曰，'天下國家。'天下之本在國，國之本在家，家之本在身。"

6. 孟子曰："為政不難，不得罪於巨室。巨室之所慕，一國慕之；

> The lesson for the Yin was not far to seek:
> It lay with the age of the Hsia.[4]

This describes well what I have said,'

[3]i.e., 'benighted' and 'tyrannical'. These names which imply extreme condemnation were, as a matter of fact, given to Emperors of the Chou Dynasty and these are mentioned in VI. A. 6.
[4]Ode 255.

3. Mencius said, 'The Three Dynasties won the Empire through benevolence and lost it through cruelty. This is true of the rise and fall, survival and collapse, of states as well. An Emperor cannot keep the Empire within the Four Seas unless he is benevolent; a feudal lord cannot preserve the altars to the gods of earth and grain unless he is benevolent; a Minister or a Counsellor cannot preserve his ancestral temple unless he is benevolent; a Gentleman or a Commoner cannot preserve his four limbs unless he is benevolent. To dislike death yet revel in cruelty is no different from drinking beyond your capacity despite your dislike of drunkenness.'

4. Mencius said, 'If others do not respond to your love with love, look into your own benevolence; if others do not respond to your attempts to govern them with order, look into your own wisdom; if others do not return your courtesy, look into your own respect. In other words, look into yourself whenever you fail to achieve your purpose. When you are correct in your person, the Empire will turn to you. The *Odes* say,

> Long may he be worthy of Heaven's Mandate,
> And seek for himself much good fortune.[5]

[5]Ode 235.

5. Mencius said, 'There is a common expression, "The Empire, the state, the family". The Empire has its basis in the state, the state in the family, and the family in one's own self.'

6. Mencius said, 'It is not difficult to govern. All one has to do is not to offend the noble families. Whatever commands the admira-

一國之所慕，天下慕之；故沛然德敎溢乎四海。"

7. 孟子曰："天下有道，小德役大德，小賢役大賢；天下無道，小役大，弱役強。斯二者，天也。順天者存，逆天者亡。齊景公曰：'旣不能令，又不受命，是絕物也。'涕出而女於吳。今也小國師大國而恥受命焉，是猶弟子而恥受命於先師也。如恥之，莫若師文王。師文王，大國五年，小國七年，必爲政於天下矣。詩云：'商之孫子，其麗不億。上帝旣命，侯于周服。侯服于周，天命靡常。殷士膚敏，祼將于京。'孔子曰：'仁不可爲衆也。夫國君好仁，天下無敵。'今也欲無敵於天下而不以仁，是猶執熱而不以濯也。詩云：'誰能執熱，逝不以濯？'

tion of the noble families will command the admiration of the whole state; whatever commands the admiration of a state will command the admiration of the Empire. Thus moral influence irresistibly fills to overflowing the whole Empire within the Four Seas.'

7. Mencius said, 'When the Way prevails in the Empire men of small virtue serve men of great virtue, men of small ability serve men of great ability. But when the Way is in disuse, the small serve the big, the weak serve the strong. Both are due to Heaven. Those who are obedient to Heaven are preserved; those who go against Heaven are annihilated. Duke Ching of Ch'i said, "Since, on the one hand, we are not in a position to dictate, and on the other, we refuse to be dictated to, we are destined to be exterminated." With tears he gave his daughter to Wu as a bride. Now the small states emulate the big states yet feel ashamed of being dictated to by them. This is like disciples feeling ashamed of obeying their masters. If one is ashamed, the best thing is to take King Wen as one's model. He who models himself on King Wen will prevail over the whole Empire, in five years if he starts with a big state, and in seven if he starts with a small state. The *Odes* say,

> The descendants of Shang
> Exceed a hundred thousand in number,
> But because God so decreed,
> They submit to Chou.
> They submit to Chou
> Because the Mandate of Heaven is not immutable.
> The warriors of Yin are handsome and alert.
> They assist at the libations in the Chou capital.[6]

Confucius said, "Against benevolence there can be no superiority in numbers. If the ruler of a state is drawn to benevolence, he will be matchless in the Empire." Now to wish to be matchless in the Empire by any means but benevolence is like holding something hot and refusing to cool one's hand with water. The *Odes* say,

> Who can hold something hot
> And not cool his hand with water?'[7]

8.　　孟子曰："不仁者可與言哉？安其危而利其菑，樂其所以亡者。
不仁而可與言，則何亡國敗家之有？有孺子歌曰：'滄浪之水清兮，
可以濯我纓；滄浪之水濁兮，可以濯我足。'孔子曰：'小子聽之！
清斯濯纓，濁斯濯足矣。自取之也。'夫人必自侮，然後人侮之；家
必自毀，而後人毀之；國必自伐，而後人伐之。太甲曰：'天作孽，
猶可違；自作孽，不可活。'此之謂也。"

9.　　孟子曰："桀紂之失天下也，失其民也；失其民者，失其心也。
得天下有道：得其民，斯得天下矣；得其民有道：得其心，斯得民
矣；得其心有道：所欲與之聚之，所惡勿施，爾也。民之歸仁也，猶
水之就下、獸之走壙也。故為淵敺魚者，獺也；為叢敺爵者，鸇也；
為湯武敺民者，桀與紂也。今天下之君有好仁者，則諸侯皆為之敺
矣。雖欲無王，不可得已。今之欲王者，猶七年之病求三年之艾也。
苟為不畜，終身不得。苟不志於仁，終身憂辱，以陷於死亡。詩云，
'其何能淑，載胥及溺。'此之謂也。"

[6]Ode 235.
[7]Ode 257.

8. Mencius said, 'How can one get the cruel man to listen to reason? He dwells happily in danger, looks upon disaster as profitable and delights in what will lead him to perdition. If the cruel man listened to reason, there would be no annihilated states or ruined families. There was a boy who sang,

> If the blue water is clear
> It is fit to wash my chin-strap.
> If the blue water is muddy
> It is only fit to wash my feet.

Confucius said, "Listen to this, my young friends. When clear the water washes the chin-strap, when muddy it washes the feet. The water brings this difference in treatment upon itself." Only when a man invites insult will others insult him. Only when a family invites destruction will others destroy it. Only when a state invites invasion will others invade it. The *T'ai chia* says,

> When Heaven sends down calamities,
> There is hope of weathering them;
> When man brings them upon himself,
> There is no hope of escape.[8]

This describes well what I have said.'

[8]This passage from the lost *T'ai chia* is again quoted in II. A. 4.

9. Mencius said, 'It was through losing the people that Chieh and Tchou lost the Empire, and through losing the people's hearts that they lost the people. There is a way to win the Empire; win the people and you will win the Empire. There is a way to win the people; win their hearts and you will win the people. There is a way to win their hearts; amass what they want for them; do not impose what they dislike on them. That is all. The people turn to the benevolent as water flows downwards or as animals head for the wilds. Thus the otter drives the fish to the deep; thus the hawk drives birds to the bushes; and thus Chieh and Tchou drove the people to T'ang and King Wu. Now if a ruler in the Empire

10.　孟子曰：“自暴者，不可與有言也；自棄者，不可與有爲也。言非禮義，謂之自暴也；吾身不能居仁由義，謂之自棄也。仁，人之安宅也；義，人之正路也。曠安宅而弗居，舍正路而不由，哀哉！”

11.　孟子曰：“道在邇而求諸遠，事在易而求諸難；人人親其親、長其長，而天下平。”

12.　孟子曰：“居下位而不獲於上，民不可得而治也。獲於上有道，不信於友，弗獲於上矣。信於友有道，事親弗悅，弗信於友矣。悅親有道，反身不誠，不悅於親矣。誠身有道，不明乎善，不誠其身矣。是故誠者，天之道也；思誠者，人之道也。至誠而不動者，未之有也；不誠，未有能動者也。”

is drawn to benevolence, all the feudal lords will drive the people
to him. He cannot but be a true King. In the present day, those
who want to be king are like a man with an illness that has lasted
seven years seeking *ai*[9] that has been stored for three years. If one
has not the foresight to put such a thing by, one will not be able to
find it when the need arises. If one does not aim steadfastly at
benevolence, one will suffer worry and disgrace all one's life and
end in the snare of death. The *Odes* say,

> How can they be good?
> They only lead one another to death by drowning.[10]

This describes well what I have said.'

[9]*Ai* is a herb of the genus Artemisia. In a dried form it is burned close to the skin as a
treatment for certain ailments. The method is known as *chiu* in Chinese, but is generally
known in the West as moxibustion, a term derived from the word moxa which, in turn,
is an Anglicized form of the Japanese word *mokusa*, the meaning of which is *moegusa*
(burned herb).
[10]Ode 257.

10. Mencius said, 'It is not worth the trouble to talk to a man who
has no respect for himself, and it is not worth the trouble to make
a common effort with a man who has no confidence in himself.
The former attacks morality; the latter says, "I do not think I am
capable of abiding by benevolence or of following rightness."
Benevolence is man's peaceful abode and rightness his proper path.
It is indeed lamentable for anyone not to live in his peaceful abode
and not to follow his proper path.'

11. Mencius said, 'The Way lies at hand yet it is sought afar; the
thing lies in the easy yet it is sought in the difficult. If only everyone loved his parents and treated his elders with deference, the
Empire would be at peace.

12. Mencius said, 'If a man in a subordinate position fails to win
the confidence of his superiors, he cannot hope to govern the
people. There is a way for him to win the confidence of his superiors. If his friends do not trust him, he will not win the confidence
of his superiors. There is a way for him to win the trust of his
friends. If in serving his parents he fails to please them, he will

13.　孟子曰：“伯夷辟紂，居北海之濱，聞文王作，興曰：‘盍歸乎來！吾聞西伯善養老者。’太公辟紂，居東海之濱，聞文王作，興曰：‘盍歸乎來！吾聞西伯善養老者。’二老者，天下之大老也，而歸之，是天下之父歸之也。天下之父歸之，其子焉往？諸侯有行文王之政者，七年之內，必爲政於天下矣。”

14.　孟子曰：“求也爲季氏宰，無能改於其德，而賦粟倍他日。孔子曰：‘求非我徒也，小子鳴鼓而攻之可也。’由此觀之，君不行仁政而富之，皆棄於孔子者也，況於爲之强戰？爭地以戰，殺人盈野；爭城以戰，殺人盈城，此所謂率土地而食人肉，罪不容於死。故善戰者服上刑，連諸侯者次之，辟草萊、任土地者次之。”

not win the trust of his friends. There is a way for him to please his parents. If upon looking within he finds that he has not been true to himself, he will not please his parents. There is a way for him to become true to himself. If he does not understand goodness he cannot be true to himself. Hence being true is the Way of Heaven; to reflect upon this is the Way of man. There has never been a man totally true to himself who fails to move others. On the other hand, one who is not true to himself can never hope to move others.'

13. Mencius said, 'Po Yi fled from Tchou and settled on the edge of the North Sea. When he heard of the rise of King Wen he stirred and said, "Why not go back? I hear that Hsi Po[11] takes good care of the aged." T'ai Kung fled from Tchou and settled on the edge of the East Sea. When he heard of the rise of King Wen he stirred and said, "Why not go back? I hear that Hsi Po takes good care of the aged."[12] These two were the grand old men of the Empire, and they turned to him. In other words, the fathers of the Empire turned to him. When the fathers of the Empire turned to him, where could the sons go? If any feudal lord practises the government of King Wen he will certainly be ruling over the Empire within seven years.'

[11] i.e., King Wen.
[12] This passage is found also in VII. A. 22.

14. Mencius said, 'While he was steward to the Chi family, Jan Ch'iu doubled the yield of taxation without being able to improve their virtue. Confucius said, "Ch'iu is no disciple of mine. You, my young friends, may attack him openly to the beating of drums."[13] From this it can be seen that Confucius rejected those who enriched rulers not given to the practice of benevolent government. How much more would he reject those who do their best to wage war on their behalf. In wars to gain land, the dead fill the plains; in wars to gain cities, the dead fill the cities. This is known as showing the land the way to devour human flesh. Death is too light a punishment for such men. Hence those skilled in war should suffer the most severe punishments; those who secure alliances with other

15. 孟子曰：“存乎人者，莫良於眸子。眸子不能掩其惡。胸中正，則眸子瞭焉；胸中不正，則眸子眊焉。聽其言也，觀其眸子，人焉廋哉？”

16. 孟子曰：“恭者不侮人，儉者不奪人。侮奪人之君，惟恐不順焉，惡得爲恭儉？恭儉豈可以聲音笑貌爲哉？”

17. 淳于髡曰：“男女授受不親，禮與？”

　　孟子曰：“禮也。”

　　曰：“嫂溺，則援之以手乎？”

　　曰：“嫂溺不援，是豺狼也。男女授受不親，禮也；嫂溺，援之以手者，權也。”

　　曰：“今天下溺矣，夫子之不援，何也？”

　　曰：“天下溺，援之以道；嫂溺，援之以手——子欲手援天下乎？”

18. 公孫丑曰：“君子之不教子，何也？”

　　孟子曰：“勢不行也。教者必以正；以正不行，繼之以怒。繼之以怒，則反夷矣。‘夫子教我以正，夫子未出於正也。’則是父子相夷也。父子相夷，則惡矣。古者易子而教之，父子之間不責善。責善則離，離則不祥莫大焉。”

feudal lords come next, and then come those who open up waste land and increase the yield of the soil.'

[13] Cf. the *Analects of Confucius*, XI. 7.

15. Mencius said, 'There is in man nothing more ingenuous than the pupils of his eyes. They cannot conceal his wickedness. When he is upright within his breast, a man's pupils are clear and bright; when he is not, they are clouded and murky. How can a man conceal his true character if you listen to his words and observe the pupils of his eyes?'

16. Mencius said, 'He who is respectful does not insult others; he who is frugal does not rob others. The one fear of rulers who insult and rob others is that the people will not be docile. How can they be respectful and frugal? Can an unctuous voice and a smiling countenance pass for respectfulness and frugality?'

17. Ch'un-yü K'un said, 'Is it prescribed by the rites that, in giving and receiving, man and woman should not touch each other?'

'It is,' said Mencius.

'When one's sister-in-law is drowning, does one stretch out a hand to help her?'

'Not to help a sister-in-law who is drowning is to be a brute. It is prescribed by the rites that, in giving and receiving, man and woman should not touch each other, but in stretching out a helping hand to the drowning sister-in-law one uses one's discretion.' 權

'Now the Empire is drowning. Why do you not help it?'

'When the Empire is drowning, one helps it with the Way; when a sister-in-law is drowning, one helps her with one's hand. Would you have me help the Empire with my hand?'

18. Kung-sun Ch'ou said, 'Why does a gentleman not take on the teaching of his own sons?'

'Because in the nature of things,' said Mencius, 'it will not work. A teacher necessarily resorts to correction, and if correction produces no effect, it will end by his losing his temper. When this happens, father and son will hurt each other instead. "You teach

19.　孟子曰：「事，孰爲大？事親爲大；守，孰爲大？守身爲大。不失其身而能事其親者，吾聞之矣；失其身而能事其親者，吾未之聞也。孰不爲事？事親，事之本也；孰不爲守？守身，守之本也。曾子養曾皙，必有酒肉；將徹，必請所與；問有餘，必曰，『有。』曾皙死，曾元養曾子，必有酒肉；將徹，不請所與；問有餘，曰，『亡矣。』——將以復進也。此所謂養口體者也。若曾子，則可謂養志也。事親若曾子者，可也。」

20.　孟子曰：「人不足與適也，政不足間也；惟大人爲能格君心之非。君仁，莫不仁；君義，莫不義；君正，莫不正。一正君而國定矣。」

me by correcting me, but you yourself are not correct." So father and son hurt each other, and it is bad that such a thing should happen. In antiquity people taught one another's sons. Father and son should not demand goodness from each other.[14] To do so will estrange them, and there is nothing more inauspicious than estrangement between father and son.'

[14] Cf. 'It is for friends to demand goodness from each other. For father and son to do so seriously undermines the love between them.' (IV. B. 30).

19. Mencius said, 'What is the most important duty? One's duty towards one's parents. What is the most important thing to watch over? One's own character. I have heard of a man who, not having allowed his character to be morally lost, is able to discharge his duties towards his parents; but I have not heard of one morally lost who is able to do so. There are many duties one should discharge, but the fulfilment of one's duty towards one's parents is the most basic. There are many things one should watch over, but watching over one's character is the most basic.

'Tseng Tzu, in looking after Tseng Hsi,[15] saw to it that he always had meat and drink, and, on clearing away the food, always asked to whom it should be given. When asked whether there was any food left, he always replied in the affirmative. After Tseng Hsi's death, when Tseng Yüan looked after Tseng Tzu, he, too, saw to it that he always had meat and drink, but, on clearing away the food, never asked to whom it should be given. When asked whether there was any food left, he always replied in the negative. He did this so that the left-over food could be served up again. This can only be described as looking after the mouth and belly. Someone like Tseng Tzu can truly be said to be solicitous of the wishes of his parent. One does well if one can emulate the way Tseng Tzu treated his parent.'

[15] This is the father of Tseng Tzu, not to be confused with the Tseng Hsi who was Tseng Tzu's younger son. See note to II. A. 1.

20. Mencius said, 'The people in power are not worth our censure; their government is not worth condemnation. The great man alone can rectify the evils in the prince's heart. When the prince is benevolent, everyone else is benevolent; when the prince is dutiful,

21. 孟子曰：「有不虞之譽，有求全之毀。」

22. 孟子曰：「人之易其言也，無責耳矣。」

23. 孟子曰：「人之患在好爲人師。」

24. 樂正子從於子敖之齊。
　　　　樂正子見孟子。孟子曰：「子亦來見我乎？」
　　　　曰：「先生何爲出此言也？」
　　　　曰：「子來幾日矣？」
　　　　曰：「昔者。」
　　　　曰：「昔者，則我出此言也，不亦宜乎？」
　　　　曰：「舍館未定。」
　　　　曰：「子聞之也，舍館定，然後求見長者乎？」
　　　　曰：「克有罪。」

25. 孟子謂樂正子曰：「子之從於子敖來，徒餔啜也。我不意子學古之道而以餔啜也。」

26. 孟子曰：「不孝有三，無後爲大。舜不告而娶，爲無後也，君子以爲猶告也。」

everyone else is dutiful; when the prince is correct, everyone else is correct. Simply by rectifying the prince one can put the state on a firm basis.'

21. Mencius said, 'There is unexpected praise; equally, there is perfectionist criticism.'

22. Mencius said, 'He who opens his mouth lightly does so simply because he has no responsibilities of office.'[16]

[16]Cf. 'People with no official positions are uninhibited in the expression of their views' (III. B. 9). The traditional interpretation of this saying is: 'A man opens his mouth lightly because he has never been taken to task for saying the wrong thing.'

23. Mencius said, 'The trouble with people is that they are too eager to assume the role of teacher.'

24. Yüeh-cheng Tzu came to Ch'i in the retinue of Tzu-ao.[17] He went to see Mencius, who said, 'It is very gracious of you to come to see me.'
   'Why do you say such a thing, sir?'
   'How many days is it since you arrived?'
   'I arrived yesterday.'
   'In that case, am I not justified in my remark?'
   'I was waiting to be settled in lodgings.'
   'Where did you learn that one should only visit one's elders after one has settled in one's lodgings?'
   'I am guilty.'

[17]i.e., Wang Huan who appears in II. B. 6 and IV. B. 27.

25. Mencius said to Yüeh-cheng Tzu, 'Have you come in the retinue of Tzu-ao solely for the sake of food and drink? I never thought that you would put the way of antiquity that you studied to such a use.'

26. Mencius said, 'There are three ways of being a bad son. The most serious is to have no heir. Shun married without telling his father for fear of not having an heir. To the gentleman, this was as

everyone else is dutiful when the prince is correct, everyone else
is content simply by rectifying the prince one can put the state on

27. 孟子曰：“仁之實，事親是也；義之實，從兄是也；智之實，知
斯二者弗去是也；禮之實，節文斯二者是也；樂之實，樂斯二者，樂
則生矣；生則惡可已也，惡可已，則不知足之蹈之手之舞之。”

28. 孟子曰：“天下大悅而將歸己，視天下悅而歸己，猶草芥也，惟
舜爲然。不得乎親，不可以爲人；不順乎親，不可以爲子。舜盡事親
之道而瞽瞍底豫，瞽瞍底豫而天下化，瞽瞍底豫而天下之爲父子者
定，此之謂大孝。”

good as having told his father.'[18]

[18]Cf. V. A. 2.

27. Mencius said, 'The content of benevolence is the serving of one's parents; the content of dutifulness is obedience to one's elder brothers; the content of wisdom is to understand these two and to hold fast to them; the content of the rites is the regulation and adornment of them; the content of music is the joy that comes of delighting in them. When joy arises how can one stop it? And when one cannot stop it, then one begins to dance with one's feet and wave one's arms without knowing it.'

28. Mencius said, 'Shun alone was able to look upon the fact that the Empire, being greatly delighted, was turning to him, as of no more consequence than trash. When one does not please one's parents, one cannot be a man; when one is not obedient to one's parents, one cannot be a son. Shun did everything that was possible to serve his parents, and succeeded, in the end, in pleasing the Blind Man.[19] Once the Blind Man was pleased, the Empire was transformed. Once the Blind Man was pleased, the pattern for the relationship between father and son in the Empire was set. This is the supreme achievement of a dutiful son.'

[19]Shun's father.

離婁章句下

1.　孟子曰：“舜生於諸馮，遷於負夏，卒於鳴條，東夷之人也，文王生於岐周，卒於畢郢，西夷之人也。地之相去也，千有餘里；世之相後也，千有餘歲。得志行乎中國，若合符節，先聖後聖，其揆一也。”

2.　子產聽鄭國之政，以其乘輿濟人於溱洧。孟子曰：“惠而不知爲政。歲十一月，徒杠成；十二月，輿梁成，民未病涉也。君子平其政，行辟人可也，焉得人人而濟之？故爲政者，每人而悅之，日亦不足矣。”

3.　孟子告齊宣王曰：“君之視臣如手足，則臣視君如腹心；君之視臣如犬馬，則臣視君如國人；君之視臣如土芥，則臣視君如寇讎。”

　　王曰：“禮，爲舊君有服，何如斯可爲服矣？”

　　曰：“諫行言聽，膏澤下於民；有故而去，則使人導之出疆，又先於其所往；去三年不反，然後收其田里。此之謂三有禮焉。如此，則爲之服矣。今也爲臣，諫則不行，言則不聽；膏澤不下於民；有故而去，則君搏執之，又極之於其所往；去之日，遂收其田里。此之謂寇讎。寇讎，何服之有？”

BOOK IV · PART B

1. Mencius said, 'Shun was an Eastern barbarian; he was born in Chu Feng, moved to Fu Hsia, and died in Ming T'iao. King Wen was a Western barbarian; he was born in Ch'i Chou and died in Pi Ying. Their native places were over a thousand *li* apart, and there were a thousand years between them. Yet when they had their way in the Central Kingdoms, their actions matched like the two halves of a tally. The standards of the two sages, one earlier and one later, were identical.'

2. When the administration of the state of Cheng was in his hands, Tzu-ch'an used his own carriage to take people across the Chen and the Wei.

'He was a generous man,' commented Mencius, 'but he did not know how to govern. If the footbridges are built by the eleventh month and the carriage bridges by the twelfth month[1] every year, the people will not suffer the hardship of fording. A gentleman, when he governs properly, may clear his path of people when he goes out. How can he find the time to take each man across the river? Hence if a man in authority has to please every one separately, he will not find the day long enough.'

[1] Equivalent to the ninth and tenth months of the present lunar calendar. See note to I. A. 6.

3. Mencius said to King Hsüan of Ch'i, 'If a prince treats his subjects as his hands and feet, they will treat him as their belly and heart. If he treats them as his horses and hounds, they will treat him as a mere fellow-countryman. If he treats them as mud and weeds, they will treat him as an enemy.'

'According to the rites,' said the King, 'there is provision for wearing mourning for a prince one has once served. Under what circumstances will this be observed?'

'When a subject whose advice has been adopted to the benefit of the people has occasion to leave the country, the prince sends someone to conduct him beyond the border, and a messenger is

4.　孟子曰：“無罪而殺士，則大夫可以去；無罪而戮民，則士可以徙。”

5.　孟子曰：“君仁，莫不仁；君義，莫不義。”

6.　孟子曰：“非禮之禮，非義之義，大人弗爲。”

7.　孟子曰：“中也養不中，才也養不才，故人樂有賢父兄也。如中也棄不中，才也棄不才，則賢不肖之相去，其間不能以寸。”

8.　孟子曰：“人有不爲也，而後可以有爲。”

9.　孟子曰：“言人之不善，當如後患何？”

10.　孟子曰：“仲尼不爲已甚者。”

sent ahead to prepare the way. Only if, after three years, he decides not to return does the prince take over his land. This is known as the three courtesies. If the prince behaves in this way then it is the subject's duty to wear mourning for him. Today when a subject whose advice has been rejected to the detriment of the people has occasion to leave, the prince has him arrested and put in chains, makes things difficult for him in the state he is going to and appropriates his land the day he leaves. This is what is meant by "enemy". What mourning is there for an enemy?'

4. Mencius said, 'When an innocent Gentleman is put to death, a Counsellor is justified in leaving; when innocent people are killed, a Gentleman is justified in going to live abroad.'

5. Mencius said, 'When the prince is benevolent, everyone else is benevolent; when the prince is dutiful, everyone else is dutiful.'[2]

[2] This saying forms part of IV. A. 20.

6. Mencius said, 'A great man will not observe a rite that is contrary to the spirit of the rites, nor will he perform a duty that goes against the spirit of dutifulness.'

7. Mencius said, 'Those who are morally well-adjusted look after those who are not; those who are talented look after those who are not. That is why people are glad to have good fathers and elder brothers. If those who are morally well-adjusted and talented abandon those who are not, then scarcely an inch will separate the good from the depraved.'

8. Mencius said, 'Only when there are things a man will not do is he capable of doing great things.'

9. Mencius said, 'Think of the consequences before you speak of the shortcomings of others.'

10. Mencius said, 'Confucius was a man who never went beyond reasonable limits.'

11.　孟子曰：“大人者，言不必信，行不必果，惟義所在。”

12.　孟子曰：“大人者，不失其赤子之心者也。”

13.　孟子曰：“養生者不足以當大事，惟送死可以當大事。”

14.　孟子曰：“君子深造之以道，欲其自得之也。自得之，則居之安；居之安，則資之深；資之深，則取之左右逢其原，故君子欲其自得之也。”

15.　孟子曰：“博學而詳說之，將以反說約也。”

16.　孟子曰：“以善服人者，未有能服人者也；以善養人，然後能服天下。天下不心服而王者，未之有也。”

17.　孟子曰：“言無實不祥。不祥之實，蔽賢者當之。”

18.　徐子曰：“仲尼亟稱於水，曰‘水哉，水哉！’何取於水也？”
　　　孟子曰：“源泉混混，不舍晝夜，盈科而後進，放乎四海。有本者如是，是之取爾。苟爲無本，七八月之間雨集，溝澮皆盈；其涸也，可立而待也。故聲聞過情，君子恥之。”

11. Mencius said, 'A great man need not keep his word nor does he necessarily see his action through to the end. He aims only at what is right.'

12. Mencius said, 'A great man is one who retains the heart of a new-born babe.'

13. Mencius said, 'Keeping one's parents when they are alive is not worth being described as of major importance; it is treating them decently when they die that is worth such a description.'

14. Mencius said, 'A gentleman steeps himself in the Way because he wishes to find it in himself. When he finds it in himself, he will be at ease in it; when he is at ease in it, he can draw deeply upon it; when he can draw deeply upon it, he finds its source wherever he turns. That is why a gentleman wishes to find the Way in himself.'

15. Mencius said, 'Learn widely and go into what you have learned in detail so that in the end you can return to the essential.'

16. Mencius said, 'You can never succeed in winning the allegiance of men by trying to dominate them through goodness. You can only succeed by using this goodness for their welfare. You can never gain the Empire without the heart-felt admiration of the people in it.'

17. Mencius said, 'Words without reality are ill-omened, and the reality of the ill-omened will befall those who stand in the way of good people.'

18. Hsü Tzu said, 'More than once Confucius expressed his admiration for water by saying, "Water! Oh, water!"[3] What was it he saw in water?'

'Water from an ample source,' said Mencius, 'comes tumbling down, day and night without ceasing, going forward only after all the hollows are filled,[4] and then draining into the sea. Anything that has an ample source is like that. What Confucius saw in water is just this and nothing more. If a thing has no source, it is like the

19. 孟子曰：“人之所以異於禽獸者幾希，庶民去之，君子存之。舜明於庶物，察於人倫，由仁義行，非行仁義也。”

20. 孟子曰：“禹惡旨酒而好善言。湯執中，立賢無方。文王視民如傷，望道而未之見。武王不泄邇，不忘遠。周公思兼三王，以施四事；其有不合者，仰而思之，夜以繼日；幸而得之，坐以待旦。”

21. 孟子曰：“王者之迹熄而詩亡，詩亡然後春秋作。晉之乘，楚之檮杌，魯之春秋，一也：其事則齊桓、晉文，其文則史。孔子曰：‘其義則丘竊取之矣。’”

rain water that collects after a downpour in the seventh and eighth months.[5] It may fill all the gutters, but we can stand and wait for it to dry up. Thus a gentleman is ashamed of an exaggerated reputation.'

[3] Cf. the *Analects of Confucius*, IX. 17.
[4] Cf. VII. A. 24.
[5] Equivalent to the fifth and sixth months in the present lunar calendar. See note to I. A. 6.

19. Mencius said, 'Slight is the difference between man and the brutes. The common man loses this distinguishing feature, while the gentleman retains it. Shun understood the way of things and had a keen insight into human relationships. He followed the path of morality. He did not just put morality into practice.'

20. Mencius said, 'Yü disliked delicious wine but was fond of good advice. T'ang held to the mean, and adhered to no fixed formula in the selection of able men. King Wen treated the people as if he were tending invalids, and gazed at the Way as if he had never seen it before. King Wu never treated those near him with familiarity, nor did he forget those who were far away. The Duke of Chou sought to combine the achievements of the Three Dynasties and the administrations of the Four Kings. Whenever there was anything he could not quite understand, he would tilt his head back and reflect, if need be, through the night as well as the day. If he was fortunate enough to find the answer, he would sit up to await the dawn.'

21. Mencius said, 'After the influence of the true King came to an end, songs were no longer collected. When songs were no longer collected, the *Spring and Autumn Annals* were written. The *Sheng* of Chin, the *T'ao U* of Ch'u and the *Spring and Autumn Annals* of Lu are the same kind of work. The events recorded concern Duke Huan of Ch'i and Duke Wen of Chin, and the style is that of the official historian. Confucius said, "I have appropriated the didactic principles therein." '

22. 孟子曰：“君子之澤五世而斬，小人之澤五世而斬。予未得爲孔子徒也，予私淑諸人也。”

23. 孟子曰：“可以取，可以無取，取傷廉；可以與，可以無與，與傷惠；可以死，可以無死，死傷勇。”

24. 逢蒙學射於羿，盡羿之道，思天下惟羿爲愈己，於是殺羿。孟子曰：“是亦羿有罪焉。”

　　“公明儀曰：‘宜若無罪焉。’”

　　曰：“薄乎云爾，惡得無罪？鄭人使子濯孺子侵衞，衞使庾公之斯追之。子濯孺子曰：‘今日我疾作，不可以執弓，吾死矣夫！’問其僕曰：‘追我者誰也？’其僕曰：‘庾公之斯也。’曰：‘吾生矣。’其僕曰：‘庾公之斯，衞之善射者也；夫子曰吾生，何謂也？’曰：‘庾公之斯學射於尹公之他，尹公之他學射於我。夫尹公之他，端人也，其取友必端矣。’庾公之斯至，曰：‘夫子何爲不執弓？’曰：‘今日我疾作，不可以執弓。’曰：‘小人學射於尹公之他，尹公之他學射於夫子。我不忍以夫子之道反害夫子。雖然，今日之事，君事也，我不敢廢。’抽矢，扣輪，去其金，發乘矢而後反。”

25. 孟子曰：“西子蒙不潔，則人皆掩鼻而過之；雖有惡人，齋戒沐浴，則可以祀上帝。”

22. Mencius said, 'The influence of both the gentleman and the small men ceases to be felt after five generations. I have not had the good fortune to have been a disciple of Confucius. I have learned indirectly from him through others.'

23. Mencius said, 'When it is permissible both to accept and not to accept, it is an abuse of integrity to accept. When it is permissible both to give and not to give, it is an abuse of generosity to give. When it is permissible both to die and not to die, it is an abuse of valour to die.'

24. P'eng Meng learned archery from Yi, and, having learned everything Yi could teach, thought to himself that in all the world Yi was the only archer better than himself. Thereupon he killed Yi.
    'Yi,' commented Mencius, 'was also to blame.'
    'Kung-ming Yi said, "It would seem that he was not to blame." '
    'All Kung-ming Yi meant was that the blame was slight, but how can Yi be said to be blameless? The men of Cheng sent Tzu-chuo Ju-tzu to invade Wei, and Wei sent Yü Kung chih Ssu to pursue him. Tzu-chuo Ju-tzu said, "I have an attack of an old complaint today and cannot hold my bow. I suppose I am as good as dead." He then asked his driver, "Who is pursuing me?" His driver said, "Yü Kung chih Ssu." "Then I shall not die." His driver said, "Yü Kung chih Ssu is the best archer in Wei. Why do you say, 'Then I shall not die'?" "Yü Kung chih Ssu learned archery from Yin Kung chih T'uo who learned it from me. Yin Kung chih T'uo is an upright man and I have no doubt that he chooses only upright men as his friends." Yü Kung chih Ssu came up and said, "Master, why have you not taken up your bow?" "I have an attack of an old complaint today and cannot hold my bow." "I learned archery from Yin Kung chih T'uo who learned it from you. I cannot bring myself to harm you by your own art. Nevertheless, what I am charged with today is the affair of my prince. I dare not neglect it." He drew his arrows, knocked their tips off against the wheel, and let fly a set of four arrows before he retired.'

25. Mencius said, 'If the beauty Hsi Shih is covered with filth, then people will hold their noses when they pass her. But should an

26. 孟子曰：“天下之言性也，則故而已矣。故者以利爲本。所惡於智者，爲其鑿也。如智者若禹之行水也，則無惡於智矣。禹之行水也，行其所無事也。如智者亦行其所無事，則智亦大矣。天之高也，星辰之遠也，苟求其故，千歲之日至，可坐而致也。”

27. 公行子有子之喪，右師往弔。入門，有進而與右師言者，有就右師之位而與右師言者。孟子不與右師言，右師不悅曰：“諸君子皆與驩言，孟子獨不與驩言，是簡驩也。”

　　孟子聞之，曰：“禮，朝廷不歷位而相與言，不踰階而相揖也。我欲行禮，子敖以我爲簡，不亦異乎？”

28. 孟子曰：“君子所以異於人者，以其存心也。君子以仁存心，以禮存心。仁者愛人，有禮者敬人。愛人者，人恆愛之；敬人者，人恆敬之。有人於此，其待我以橫逆，則君子必自反也：我必不仁也，必無禮也，此物奚宜至哉？其自反而仁矣，自反而有禮矣，其橫逆由是也，君子必自反也，我必不忠。自反而忠矣，其橫逆由是也，君子曰：‘此亦妄人也已矣。如此，則與禽獸奚擇哉？於禽獸又何難焉？’是

ugly[6] man fast and cleanse himself, he would be fit to offer
sacrifices to God.'

[6] Mencius is here playing on the fact that the word *e* means 'evil' as well as 'ugly'.

26. Mencius said, 'In the theories about human nature put forth by
the world there is nothing else other than resort to precedents. The
primary thing in any resort to precedents is ease of explanation.
What one dislikes in clever men is their tortuosity. If clever men
could act as Yü did in guiding the flood waters, then there would
be nothing to dislike in them. Yü guided the water by imposing
nothing on it that was against its natural tendency. If clever men
can also do this, then great indeed will their cleverness be. In spite
of the height of the heavens and the distance of the heavenly
bodies, if one seeks out former instances, one can calculate the
solstices of a thousand years hence without stirring from one's
seat.'

27. Kung-hang Tzu lost a son, and Wang Huan, the *yu shih*.[7] went
to offer his condolences. As he entered, people went up to greet
him, and, as he sat down, others came over to speak to him.
Mencius did not speak to him and Wang Huan was displeased. 'All
the gentlemen present spoke to me,' said he, 'with the sole
exception of Mencius. He showed me scant courtesy.'

Mencius, on hearing of this, said, 'According to the rites, at
court one should not step across seats to speak to others, neither
should one step across steps to bow to them. All I wished was to
observe the rites, and Tzu-ao thought I was showing him scant
courtesy. Is that not extraordinary?'

[7] An official post in the state of Ch'i. It is not clear what its functions were.

28. Mencius said, 'A gentleman differs from other men in that he
retains his heart. A gentleman retains his heart by means of
benevolence and the rites. The benevolent man loves others, and
the courteous man respects others. He who loves others is always
loved by them; he who respects others is always respected by
them. Suppose a man treats one in an outrageous manner. Faced
with this, a gentleman will say to himself, "I must be lacking in

故君子有終身之憂，無一朝之患也。乃若所憂則有之：舜，人也；我，亦人也。舜爲法於天下，可傳於後世，我由未免爲鄉人也，是則可憂也。憂之如何？如舜而已矣。若夫君子所患則亡矣。非仁無爲也，非禮無行也。如有一朝之患，則君子不患矣。」

29. 禹、稷當平世，三過其門而不入，孔子賢之。顏子當亂世，居於陋巷，一簞食，一瓢飲；人不堪其憂，顏子不改其樂，孔子賢之。孟子曰：「禹、稷、顏回同道。禹思天下有溺者，由己溺之也；稷思天下有飢者，由己飢之也，是以如是其急也。禹、稷、顏子易地則皆然。今有同室之人鬬者，救之，雖被髮纓冠而救之，可也；鄉鄰有鬬者，被髮纓冠而往救之，則惑也；雖閉戶可也。」

benevolence and courtesy, how else could such a thing happen to me?" When, looking into himself, he finds that he has been benevolent and courteous, and yet this outrageous treatment continues, then the gentleman will say to himself, "I must have failed to do my best for him." When, on looking into himself, he finds that he has done his best and yet this outrageous treatment continues, then the gentleman will say, "This man does not know what he is doing. Such a person is no different from an animal. One cannot expect an animal to know any better." Hence while a gentleman has perennial worries, he has no unexpected vexations. His worries are of this kind. Shun was a man; I am also a man. Shun set an example for the Empire worthy of being handed down to posterity, yet here am I, just an ordinary man. That is something worth worrying about. If one worries about it, what should one do? One should become like Shun. That is all. On the other hand, the gentleman is free from vexations. He never does anything that is not benevolent; he does not act except in accordance with the rites. Even when unexpected vexations come his way, the gentleman refuses to be vexed.'

29. In a period of peace, Yü and Chi passed their own door three times without entering.[8] Confucius praised them for it. In an age of disorder, Yen Hui lived in a mean dwelling on a bowlful of rice and a ladleful of water. This is a hardship most men would find in supportable, but Yen Tzu did not allow this to affect his joy. Confucius also praised him for it.[9]

'The way followed by Yü, Chi and Yen Hui,' commented Mencius, 'was the same. Yü looked upon himself as responsible for anyone in the Empire who drowned; Chi looked upon himself as responsible for anyone in the Empire who starved.[10] That is why they went about their tasks with such a sense of urgency. Had Yü, Chi and Yen Hui changed places they would not have acted differently.

'Now if a fellow-lodger is involved in a fight, it is right for you to rush to his aid with your hair hanging down and your cap untied. But it would be misguided to do so if it were only a fellow-villager. There is nothing wrong with bolting your door.'

[8]Yü was the one who passed his door three times without entering. Chi is mentioned

30. 公都子曰：「匡章，通國皆稱不孝焉，夫子與之遊，又從而禮貌之，敢問何也？」

孟子曰：「世俗所謂不孝者五，惰其四支，不顧父母之養，一不孝也；博奕好飲酒，不顧父母之養，二不孝也；好貨財，私妻子，不顧父母之養，三不孝也；從耳目之欲，以爲父母戮，四不孝也；好勇鬥很，以危父母，五不孝也。章子有一於是乎？夫章子，子父責善而不相遇也。責善，朋友之道也；父子責善，賊恩之大者。夫章子，豈不欲有夫妻子母之屬哉？爲得罪於父，不得近，出妻屏子，終身不養焉。其設心以爲不若是，是則罪之大者，是則章子已矣。」

31. 曾子居武城，有越寇。或曰：「寇至，盍去諸？」曰：「無寓人於我室，毀傷其薪木。」寇退，則曰：「脩我牆屋，我將反。」寇退，曾子反。左右曰：「待先生如此其忠且敬也，寇至，則先去以爲民望；

here only because his name is often coupled with that of Yü. See, for instance, III. A. 4.

[9] Cf. the *Analects of Confucius*, VI. 11.

[10] because Yü was entrusted with the task of dealing with the Flood and Chi with the task of teaching the people the art of cultivating the crops. Again, see III. A. 4.

30. Kung-tu Tzu said, 'K'uang Chang is dubbed an undutiful son by the whole country. Why do you, Master, not only assoicate with him but treat him with courtesy?'

'What the world commonly calls undutiful in a son falls under five heads,' said Mencius. 'First, the neglect of one's parents through laziness of limb. Second, the neglect of one's parents through indulgence in the games of *po* and *yi* and fondness for drink. Third, the neglect of one's parents through miserliness in money matters and partiality towards one's wife. Fourth, indulgence in sensual pleasures to the shame of one's parents. Fifth, a quarrelsome and truculent disposition that jeopardizes the safety of one's parents. Has Chang Tzu a single one of these failings? In his case father and son are at odds through taxing each other over a moral issue. It is for friends to demand goodness from each other. For father and son to do so seriously undermines the love between them.[11] Do you think that Chang Tzu does not want to be with his wife and sons? Because of his offence, he is not allowed near his father. Therefore, he sent his wife and sons away and refused to allow them to look after him. To his way of thinking, unless he acted in this way, his offence would be the greater. That is Chang Tzu for you.'[12]

[11] Cf. IV. A. 18.

[12] It is not clear what transpired between K'uang Chang and his father. In the *Chan kuo ts'e* (*Ch'i ts'e* 1/13) there is an account of one Chang Tzu whose father killed his mother and buried her under the stables. Chang Tzu wanted to have his mother reburied but felt unable to do so as his father died without leaving instructions for it. Although this account has been related to the dispute referred to here by Mencius, it does not seem justified, as in the *Chan kuo ts'e* there is in fact no mention of any dispute between father and son during the time when the father was alive. It is likely that the Chang Tzu in the *Chan kuo ts'e* is not the same as the K'uang Chang here. For a discussion of this problem see Appendix I, p. 314-5).

31. Tseng Tzu lived in Wu Ch'eng. Invaders came from Yüeh. Someone said, 'Invaders are coming. Why do you not leave?'

'Do not let anyone,' said Tseng Tzu, 'live in my house or do damage to my trees.'

寇退，則反，殆於不可。"沈猶行曰："是非汝所知也。昔沈猶有負
芻之禍，從先生者七十人，未有與焉。"

子思居於衞，有齊寇。或曰："寇至，盍去諸？"子思曰："如伋
去，君誰與守？"

孟子曰："曾子、子思同道。曾子，師也，父兄也；子思，臣也，
微也。曾子、子思易地則皆然。"

32. 儲子曰："王使人瞯夫子，果有以異於人乎？"孟子曰："何以
異於人哉？堯舜與人同耳。"

33. 齊人有一妻一妾而處室者，其良人出，則必饜酒肉而後反。其妻
問所與飲食者，則盡富貴也。其妻告其妾曰："良人出，則必饜酒肉
而後反；問其與飲食者，盡富貴也，而未嘗有顯者來，吾將瞯良人之
所之也。"

蚤起，施從良人之所之，徧國中無與立談者。卒之東郭墦間，之
祭者，乞其餘；不足，又顧而之他——此其爲饜足之道也。

其妻歸，告其妾，曰："良人者，所仰望而終身也，今若此——"
與其妾訕其良人，而相泣於中庭，而良人未之知也，施施從外來，驕
其妻妾。

由君子觀之，則人之所以求富貴利達者，其妻妾不羞也，而不相
泣者，幾希矣。

When the invaders left, Tseng Tzu again said, 'Repair the walls and roof of my house. I shall return presently.'

After the invaders had left, Tseng Tzu returned. His attendants said, 'The Master has been shown every respect and everything possible is done for him. Perhaps it was not right that when we were invaded he should have taken the lead in leaving and only returned after the invaders left.'

Shen-yu Hsing said, 'This is beyond your comprehension. At one time, I had trouble in my place with a man by the name of Fu Ch'u, but none of the Master's seventy followers were involved in the incident.'

Tzu-ssu lived in Wei. There were invaders from Ch'i. Someone said, 'Invaders are coming. Why do you not leave?'

'If I leave,' answered Tzu-ssu, 'who will help the prince defend the state?'

'The way followed by Tseng Tzu and Tzu-ssu,' commented Mencius, 'was the same. Tseng Tzu was a teacher, an elder; Tzu-ssu was a subject in an insignificant position. Had Tseng Tzu and Tzu-ssu changed places they would not have acted differently.'

32. Ch'u Tzu said, 'The King sent someone to spy on you to see whether you were at all different from other people.'

'In what way,' said Mencius, 'should I be different from other people? Even Yao and Shun were the same as anyone else.'

33.[13] A man from Ch'i lived with his wife and concubine. When the good man went out, he always came back full of food and drink. His wife asked about his companions, and they all turned out to be men of wealth and consequence. His wife said to the concubine, 'When our husband goes out, he always comes back full of food and drink. When I asked about his companions, they all turned out to be men of wealth and consequence, yet we never have had a distinguished visitor. I shall spy on him to see where he really goes.'

She got up early and followed her husband everywhere he went. Not a single person in the city stopped to talk to him. In the end he went to the outskirts on the east side of the city amongst the graves. He went up to someone who was offering sacrifices to the

dead and begged for what was left over. This not being enough, he looked around and went up to another. This was how he had his food and drink.

His wife went home and said to the concubine, 'A husband is someone on whom one's whole future depends, and ours turns out like this.' Together they reviled their husband and wept in the courtyard. The husband, unaware of all this, came swaggering in to show off to his womenfolk.

In the eyes of the gentleman, few of all those who seek wealth and position fail to give their wives and concubines cause to weep with shame.

[13] It is just possible that this chapter forms a unity with the preceding one, in which case this story forms part of Mencius' answer.